RADIO 1'S

CLASSIC INTERVIEWS

25 ROCK GREATS IN THEIR OWN WORDS

Published by BBC Books,
a division of BBC Enterprises Limited,
Woodlands, 80 Wood Lane
London W12 0TT

First published 1992
© The Editor, the Interviewers and the Contributors 1992
ISBN 0 563 36408 4

Set in Monotype Twentieth Century by Ace Filmsetting Ltd, Frome
Printed and bound in Great Britain by Clays Ltd, St Ives plc
Cover printed by Clays Ltd, St Ives plc

RADIO 1'S

CLASSIC INTERVIEWS

25 ROCK GREATS IN THEIR OWN WORDS

EDITED BY JEFF SIMPSON

BBC BOOKS

To the boss
JOHNNY BEERLING

and to
DB and MF

ACKNOWLEDGEMENTS

Thanks to all the staff, presenters and producers over the years at Radio 1 who have created an archive of popular music history which is unique in the world. In particular I gratefully acknowledge the enormous help, advice and wisdom of the following: Sandy Chalmers, Paul Gambaccini, Jeff Griffin, Stuart Grundy, Kevin Howlett, Cheryl Lawrence, Phil Lawton in the Radio 1 Archive, Julia Lupton, Sue Lynas, John Pidgeon, Zowie Recche, Taryn Rock, the Radio 1 Workshop, and the BBC's audio-video transcribing service, SoundScript.

All the musicians featured in this book have kindly agreed to donate their fee to various charities, including the Prince's Trust and the Terrence Higgins Trust.

ABBA interview included courtesy of Bocu Music.

Jeff Simpson, a graduate of the University of London, worked for an international public relations consultancy before joining the BBC's Corporate Affairs Division in 1986. As Press and Publicity Officer for Radio 1, he has been involved in projects ranging from the first major broadcast initiative on AIDS in December 1986 to the Nelson Mandela birthday tribute and Knebworth 90 concerts. He has also been involved in a number of the recordings later selected as *Classic Interviews*.

CONTENTS

INTRODUCTION

BY PAUL GAMBACCINI

We are nothing without them. As our beloved mentor Alan Freeman has said several times, disc jockeys can only be as good as the music they play. Were it not for the artists whose words you are about to read, Tony Blackburn and John Peel, Noel Edmonds and Simon Mayo might have been at the labour exchange long ago.

Our interest in these music makers extends beyond listening to their work. We want to hear them talk. Can Freddie Mercury's speaking voice really have been so different from his recorded persona? Can ABBA, who sound so carefree in their songs, really be so serious in real life? And it isn't just how they sound that we want to hear. We want to hear what they have to say — the stories behind the songs, the experiences building up to the creation of their music.

It was not always this way. Until just before Radio 1 came on air in 1967, it was assumed teen idols had nothing of interest to say other than details of their personal tastes, be it their favourite colour or their preferred make of automobile. They could not talk about the genesis of their work had they been asked, because the first great stars of the rock era, with a few notable exceptions, did not write their own material. It took the Beatles to make the world not only interested in but obsessed with the creative process of the stars and their private thoughts on public issues. (Bob Dylan, whose initial songwriting successes preceded the Beatle breakthrough in America, might have earned this distinction, but he was a notoriously indifferent interviewee. Of the hundreds of people I have interviewed professionally, he was the most disappointing.)

Radio 1 quickly came to be the outlet through which musicians gave their finest broadcast interviews. Radio was always willing to devote more time to popular music than television, and when TV did offer time it tended to want performance, not chat. Commercial radio did not exist in the UK for the first several years of Radio 1's being. However, not long after its arrival it signalled its lack of interest in setting aside special slots for documentaries. They were too expensive and they interfered with the consistent station sound. The fact that almost all the significant pop music documentaries of the last quarter century have been produced by Radio 1 is one of the great arguments against a radical shake-up in its funding. Radio 1's star interviews were always more respectfully and intelligently presented than their American counterparts, which tended to be edited carelessly and aired in a slick package. In the States, commercial radio is exactly what it says — commercial first and radio second.

Radio 1 presented the first serious study of rock music to be broadcast in Britain, *The Story of Pop*. It transmitted the first multi-part series on leading groups, saluting in sequence The Beatles, The Rolling Stones and The Beach Boys. I had the great privilege of working with producer Teddy Warrick on the first multi-part study of an individual star, *The Elton John Story* in 1976, and the pleasure of presenting *The Bee Gees Story* at the height of their fame in 1978. You will find words from artists of this stature throughout this book.

But of equal pleasure to interviewers like myself, and to listeners with a wide range of interests, has been the opportunity to talk with major talents of moderate success. To bring to a British audience the words of artists like Jerry Butler and Tom Rush, people who might otherwise have gone unheard, seems to me one of the reasons I was born.

For all of us who have carted tape recorders around the world in service of Radio 1, the memories are many and precious. I treasure the thought of Luciano Pavarotti saying he has to lose weight, the very moment he is scoffing a cream cake. Somewhere out in the cosmos, hurtling at the speed of light towards the outskirts of the universe, Bonnie Raitt is begging me to ask a cab driver speeding down Fifth Avenue at 50 miles per hour to slow down before we crash. Paul McCartney is explaining that 'Jet' was a puppy. Placido Domingo is enthusing about how excited he is to have sung with John Denver. John Lydon, whom I am almost terrified to meet in his first post-Sex Pistols interview, introduces himself with the less-than-frightening words 'I saw you on telly'. Bob Marley, quietly and solemnly, is explaining the certainties of his religious faith.

The interviewers whose questions you see in these pages are united in their enthusiasm for their job. We are the intermediaries, the people who pass messages and music back and forth between artist and audience. We are, basically, some of the luckiest men and women on earth. And one of us is a subject himself – John Peel, the single individual who has had the greatest influence on popular music in Britain in the last twenty-five years.

Perhaps in 2017 Radio 1 will be able to assemble another anthology like this. It is also possible that the interest in the thoughts of star musicians will have declined to the pre-Beatles level as the public look for what Jimi Hendrix might call 'a new gas'. This book would then represent an eccentric era in the history of recorded sound. Either way, *Classic Interviews* is one of the best possible souvenirs of Radio 1's 25th anniversary. These are the people without whom we would have been nothing.

PAUL GAMBACCINI

London, 1992

1970

JIMI HENDRIX

SCENE AND HEARD, *Radio 1's rock magazine programme, had a special edition in August 1970 celebrating the Isle of Wight Festival. All the line-up were included in the programme, apart from Jimi Hendrix. Producer Jeff Griffin was determined to speak to Hendrix, who eventually agreed to talk to one of the programme's contributors, Keith Altham.*

Keith spoke to Hendrix in a hotel in London's Park Lane on 12 September. Jimi's bassist, Billy Cox, had just flown back to the States with drug problems.

'Jimi was sprawled on a double bed, with my tape recorder balanced on the other end,' recalls Altham. 'I think he may have been drinking, but there was no evidence of the drugs which everyone talks about in connection with Hendrix. Although it was two days before his death, he didn't strike me as being particularly down or depressed in any way.

'He could turn on this amazing exhibitionism on stage, but off stage he was extremely shy and introverted, so he was never especially lively in an interview situation. He was extraordinarily popular at that time, especially in America, but he was still more famous for his wild antics on stage than for his musicianship. I think he'd reached the stage where he'd made enough money, and now he wanted to push the barriers back further and extend himself a bit further. In fact I found him in fairly optimistic mood, with all kinds of plans for the future.

Very little of this interview has ever been broadcast, simply because of the way Hendrix talks in it, rambling slightly, often mumbling and laughing. He was found dead two days after it was recorded.

ALTHAM: Everybody, subsequent to the Isle of Wight Festival, has been talking about the new subdued, mature Jimi Hendrix. I wonder if you could tell us why this is, and where it started from.

HENDRIX: This is a period when I stop talking so much, because I'm going through certain things here and there. Whatever. I guess I just got very quiet for a while. I just do the gigs, and stay down. I try to stay away, you know. Because I was changing, and getting into heavier music. It was getting unbearable with three pieces [in the band], you know. I always wanted to expand on all this. But I think I'll go back to three pieces again now. And get another bass player. And I'll probably be loud again. [LAUGHS]

'JIMI WAS SPRAWLED ON A DOUBLE BED, WITH MY TAPE RECORDER BALANCED ON THE OTHER END,'
REMEMBERS KEITH ALTHAM

ALTHAM: It does appear that the days of the baubles and bangles and the freaky hairstyle have disappeared. Are you not worried that maybe your quieter approach now may lose a little of the mystique that there was with Jimi Hendrix which attracted people to begin with?

HENDRIX: You see, everybody goes through those stages. But I don't know, I just did that because I felt like I was being too loud. Because my nature just changes, you know.

ALTHAM: You were quoted in one paper as saying you never wanted to be a visual thing.

HENDRIX: What I wanted to be basically — this is only hyped up on all the visual thing — I wanted to be listened to. I don't know if they were [listening] or not, though. After a while, I started getting aware too much of what was going down. That started to bring me down a little bit, so I just started cutting my hair, and start the rings disappearing one by one.

ALTHAM: Are you in fact saying that that kind of freak thing was really a publicity hype?

HENDRIX: No. No, all they did is let me do what I really wanted to do, my own kind of scenes. Like, one time I said, 'Maybe I should burn a guitar tonight, I really feel low.' Or, 'Maybe I should smash a guitar', or something like that. And they said, 'Yeah, yeah', and I said, 'Do you really think I should?' They said, 'Yeah, that would be cool', so I said, 'OK'. So I just had to work up enough anger as to where I could do it. But I didn't take too much of the hype scene and all that, because I dug wearing all those different things. It was fun. And I still do, but I don't see where many other people are doing it, so it gives me a dumb or stupid tendency to hold back on my own desires and so forth.

ALTHAM: So the anger, maybe, has dispersed a little bit.

HENDRIX: I didn't know it was anger until they told me that it was, you know, like with destruction and all that. I believe everybody should have a room where they get rid of all their . . . releases, where they can do all their releases. So my room was a stage.

ALTHAM: What is going to happen now? You apparently said after the Isle of Wight festival that you were going to do less personal appearances.

HENDRIX: I think it can't work if we did less personal appearances. We're trying to get a tour of England together now. That's definitely going to call for another bass player.

ALTHAM: Would it be practical for you to get together maybe an organist, or a vocalist, so that you can step back as a guitarist?

HENDRIX: That's exactly what I want to do, actually. All I'll do is probably get two guitarists, counting myself, an organist and a singer. And drums, quite naturally, and bass. If I can get something like that, that would be out of sight.

ALTHAM: I remember talking to Alvin Lee of Ten Years After, and he said of you that you'd never really been truly appreciated or analysed as a songwriter. Do you feel that maybe your image got in the way of that? Do you feel that you've never truly been criticised as a songwriter?

HENDRIX'S LAST PUBLIC APPEARANCE, AT THE ISLE OF WIGHT FESTIVAL ON 18 AUGUST, 1970

HENDRIX: Well, probably that was a good thing, because I'm still trying to get that together. All I write is just what I feel, that's all. I don't really round it off too good, I keep it almost naked. The words are so blank and everything, they probably didn't want to get into that. When we go to play, you flick it around, you flash it around, but they don't see nothing but what their eyes see, you know, forget about their ears. I hate to be in one corner, I hate to be put as only a guitar player, or only as a songwriter, only as a tap-dancer or something. I like to fool around.

ALTHAM: **Is it important for you to achieve recognition as a songwriter?**

HENDRIX: I guess it would be if I wanted to lay back and predominantly write songs, when I can't go on stage any more.

ALTHAM: **You were quoted in one paper as saying you didn't really care what you did, as long as you 'turn people on'. What do you want to turn people on to, apart from your music? Is there any moral or political intent in the things you want to write?**

HENDRIX: I like for them to get easier in the mind a little bit, because there's too many heavy songs out nowadays. Music is getting too heavy, almost to the state of unbearable. I have this thing, 'When things get too heavy, just call me helium, the lightest gas known to man.' [LAUGHS]

ALTHAM: **So where are your inspirations for songs coming from at the present time? Where are you turning for your directions as a writer?**

HENDRIX: Right from my recent experiences. What I try to do is look at the totality of that, and give them the other half. First of all you have the experience, then you have the second half, the solution to whatever it might be, which is the use of it all. I was just trying to go through a lot of changes, so I could write the nice part about them, you know? But right now, it's taken a while.

ALTHAM: **You've been quoted as saying in the past that we're now at an end of something in music, and the next stage of popular music will change the world. Do you really believe that, or do you think that music is a reflection of the world?**

HENDRIX: It's always a reflection, but a reflection of the world is, like, blues. That's where that part of music is at. But then you get this other kind of music that's trying to come around — it's not sunshine music necessarily, but it's like an easier type of thing, with more meaning to it. You're not going to be singing about love all the time in order to give love to the people. I was just feeling all nice and enthusiastic when I said that. I can't go back on what I said, because that's a nice thought.

ALTHAM: **Do you want to change the world?**

HENDRIX: I'd like to take part in a change in reality, probably. Not the way to handle it, necessarily, but the way to get along a little better, as it were. Old and young don't clash so much together.

ALTHAM: **What are the things you would like to see change?**

HENDRIX: I don't know. More colour in the streets, probably. [LAUGHS] I really don't know. Whatever happens, it should have a chance to be brought into the open. If there's a new idea, a new invention, or a new gas, or a new whatever, it should be brought at least into the open, and be respected as being new, and probably a decent change that would help the human race, instead of keeping carrying the same old burdens around with them. You have to be a freak in order to be different, and even freaks, they're very prejudiced. You have to have your hair long and talk in a certain way in order to be with them. In order to be the other, you have to have your hair short and wear ties. So we're trying to make a third world happen, you know what I mean.

ALTHAM: **I think certain people think of your music as angry music, raging against establishment principles.**

HENDRIX: It's raging against it. If it was up to me there wouldn't be any such thing as the establishment. Reality is each person's way of thinking, and the establishment grabs a big piece of that, and the Church of England and so forth. But it's the blues, that's what I'm singing about, today's blues.

ALTHAM: **Do you have any politics, in fact?**

HENDRIX: Not really. I was getting ready to get into all that, but everybody goes through those stages too. It all comes out in the music, most of the time. We had this one song called 'Straight Ahead', and it says 'Power to the people, freedom to the soul, pass it on to the young and old. We don't give a damn if your hair is short or long, communication's coming on strong.'

ALTHAM: **When you look back on things like 'Hey Joe' now, how do you feel about those musically?**

HENDRIX: I think they're all right, I guess. I don't have anything to regret at all in the past. Except that I might have unintentionally hurt somebody else, or something. And the music, I think that they're all on a kind of downbeat. I just look at them as changes.

ALTHAM: **It has been said of you, that you invented psychedelic music . . .**

HENDRIX: [LAUGHS] A mad scientist!

ALTHAM: . . . Do you think that's fair? Do you think of yourself as a psychedelic writer?

HENDRIX: I think it's more that than anything else. I'm trying to get more into other things. I don't know what that word means, really. What is it? You say one thing, and mean another? Or you can get about three different meanings out of one thing? Is that where that's at?

ALTHAM: I think psychedelic to most people has connotations of LSD.

HENDRIX: You mean strictly LSD, or that type of consciousness?

ALTHAM: . . . with dreams . . . .

HENDRIX: Right. You have to get a little bit of a dream on, so you can hear it over again, because it might come in a different mood. Dreams come from different moods.

ALTHAM: You've talked quite a bit about audio-visual importance, the importance of having a film with your music. Are you thinking in terms of the days when we can fit a cassette into the side of our television and play music and film together?

HENDRIX: A lot of people are making more money than they ever had nowadays, like when they get a flat they find themselves with an extra room. So this whole room can be a total audio-visual environment, where you just lay back and the whole thing just blossoms out, with this colour and sound type of scene. You can go in here and you can just jingle out your nerves or something. That goes with a cassette, yeah. You put in your favourite star, and all of a sudden, the music and the visual scene comes on. Plus on stage, if we ever did any more stage things with this new band, it would definitely have to be audio-visual. There would probably only be about 5000 people at the performance. Because we'd have this geodesic dome. It would probably take about three days to set the whole thing up. Then you get a performance under that for the next three days. And just handfuls of people coming in. I think that would be dynamite, because everybody would get more of an effect from it. Instead of putting a big black screen behind you.

ALTHAM: What about the subject of festivals? Do you think the Isle of Wight is, as some people have said, the last big festival?

HENDRIX: I don't know why they're always trying to kill the festivals really. It was great. People milling about, digging each other, so many mixtures of different countries. The only hostility you're going to get from the festivals is not from the people themselves, but from the other people who can't understand the idea of mixing so many different people together, under the name of music, peace and love.

JIMI HENDRIX SPOKE TO RADIO 1'S *SCENE AND HEARD* IN SEPTEMBER 1970

Because this is completely different from the World War II set-up. In World War II, all these countries were completely against each other. Now we're getting them all together through the idea of music.

ALTHAM: **Do you feel personally that you've got enough money now, without necessarily making more money as a professional entertainer?**

HENDRIX: I don't think so, not the way I'd like to live.-I want to get up in the morning and roll out of my bed into an indoor swimming pool. Then swim to the breakfast table, come up for air and get maybe a drink of orange juice. And just flop over from the chair into the swimming pool and swim into the bathroom.

ALTHAM: **You don't want to live just comfortably, you want to live luxuriously.**

HENDRIX: No. Is that luxurious? I was thinking about a tent, baby, overhanging a mountain stream. [LAUGHS]

ALTHAM: **Now Billy Cox [Jimi Hendrix Experience member] has split. So whatever happens, you've got to find a new bass player. Do you intend to form another small unit, or are you hoping to get something bigger together?**

HENDRIX: I don't know. I think I'll get another small one together. It's really hard to decide. I'd like to have both if I could. And use one for touring, and then sometimes I could do a tour with a big one, or whatever. But it's really hard to know what people want around here sometimes. All I'm going to do is I'm just going to do what I feel, but right now I can't feel anything. There's a few things since this happened, so I just have to lay back and think about it all.

ALTHAM: **Do you feel any kind of compulsion to prove yourself as 'King Guitar', which is the label that people have slapped on you?**

HENDRIX: I don't know. I was always just playing loud, that's the only difference. No, I don't even let that bother me. Because they say a lot of things about people that, if they let it bother them, they wouldn't even be around today. 'King Guitar'? No, that's a bit heavy.

JIMI HENDRIX ★ 1970	
SINGLES	**REACHED**
Voodoo Chile	UK No. 1
ALBUMS	**REACHED**
Band of Gypsys	US No. 5
Band of Gypsys	UK No. 6
Monterey Pop	US No. 16

18

★

1973

MICK JAGGER
AND
KEITH RICHARDS

THE ROLLING STONES STORY was the second major documentary series attempted by Radio 1. The Beatles Story had been the first in 1972, but had not included any new interviews with members of the Beatles. The following year, Radio 1 producer Jeff Griffin realised that the Rolling Stones were the next obvious subjects for the documentary treatment.

'People in those days were either great Beatles fans or great Stones fans,' he recalls, 'so we realised we would have to do a series on the Stones. But I agreed with Radio 1's management that it would only be worth doing The Rolling Stones Story if we could get new interviews with all of the band.

'They were in Los Angeles at the time, finishing off Goat's Head Soup. I did Mick at the Beverley Wilshire Hotel. It was my first time in America, and I got a great deal of help from Ian Stewart, the band's keyboard player who was known as 'the sixth Stone', who smoothed the way for me. Mick was just about the biggest rock star in the world at the time, but in a one-to-one situation he was very natural and relaxed.

'Keith usually preferred to be away from the group, so when I spoke to him, we were alone in a house he'd rented up in the Hollywood Hills. I've been involved in a number of their interviews since, and I've found that when Keith does decide to talk, he does open up more than Mick. I think it's partly because Mick has to do so many interviews, but also that Mick is slightly more wary of the pitfalls, with the press for example. Keith just tells you what he thinks. I do remember both of them were very open when we got *on to two subjects which they felt particularly strongly about — the way they'd been treated by record companies over the years, and the persecution they'd experienced over drugs.*

'This was really the first time that a Radio 1 producer had gathered interviews like this specially for a series and, thankfully, it met with enormous critical acclaim at the time. I think it really paved the way for the other documentaries which Radio 1 has since become famous for.'

MICK JAGGER

GRIFFIN: **Mick, when did you and Keith first decide that you ought to start writing your own numbers?**

JAGGER: When the Beatles were writing. Before that, we'd just done other people's numbers, like blues numbers. I don't think we'd thought of writing hit songs. The Beatles — even though people don't like giving them credit these days, because they're all sort of gone and *passé* and everything, well, almost — they were the thing at the time, and showed you could write your own stuff. At that period, everyone always just used to re-do hits or standards, like 'Money' or 'Some Other Guy'. But then you started to get the feeling that you had to write your own because you were running out of them, so we just started writing.

GRIFFIN: **It must have been difficult for people who usually performed blues numbers to start writing their own numbers.**

JAGGER: We never really wrote any blues numbers to start off with. The things we wrote were more like ballads or pop songs. They came more naturally to us, rather than writing original blues. It's very difficult to write good original blues. The first song we ever wrote was called 'It Should Be You', I think.

GRIFFIN: **How do the tours that you do now differ from the ones that you did right back at the beginning?**

JAGGER: In the beginning, we just used to do ballrooms and clubs, and always in England. Now we plan a tour like a military campaign. I don't know why, but that's how we do it. In those days, we just used to walk on and everyone used to applaud, and no one knew any better. We just played, and it was sort of funky. In some places, like Aberystwyth, it would be dead as a dodo, and in others you'd get jumped on and you could hardly play. Now we do big places, which I don't mind. We've been doing big places since 1965, like 10000 or over. You get used to that. You can't really jam or mess about or be intimate. We don't have that any more.

MICK JAGGER IN 1973, THE YEAR OF HIS CLASSIC INTERVIEW FOR RADIO 1

GRIFFIN: Can you see any appeal in doing what Zeppelin did a couple of years back, of going back to smaller venues?

JAGGER: When you play in a club, and you're playing for two hours, then you can be intimate and chat up the audience, ask them what they want to hear, make jokes, talk about the bird on the left – 'Come up here darlin'', you know. But I haven't done that for a long while. I haven't played in clubs like that since 1965.

GRIFFIN: There was discussion at one time of the Stones and the Beatles getting together for some sort of business set-up.

JAGGER: It was always my thing that we both had very large overheads, and we didn't have any managers, i.e. when Brian Epstein died, no one had any managers. You see, we had a lot of power. I don't mean that in the bad sense. There was an era in the music industry when record companies, mostly in England, they didn't really pay you anything. They were making a fortune. I mean, if you sold a million albums, they would pay you nothing, and this was accepted. They'd pay you, like, 4 per cent – of wholesale – whereas now they would pay anyone 10 per cent of retail. We were in the position of saying, 'Hey, what's this about? You're just taking everybody's bread.' And we thought if we put ourselves together, we could turn around and stop them. But it all kind of went wrong. For a start, there were too many people, five of us and four of them. I think John and I were more or less agreed, but Paul didn't want to know, and I don't blame him. And that was it. That wasn't the only reason from the Beatles' side. I don't know all that internal story, only what I read in *Rolling Stone*.

GRIFFIN: When did you finally make the decision to set up your own label?

JAGGER: Well, it wasn't really a label. It was just a licence deal with Atlantic. When we ran out of contract with Decca, we just signed with Atlantic, with a licence deal instead of just an artist's deal. It's slightly different – not much, but slightly.

GRIFFIN: There were slight disagreements with Decca, like over the cover of *Beggars Banquet*. How heavy did that weigh?

JAGGER: They just never co-operated with us. And they always co-operated with everyone else. They just treated us like children. They made a lot of bread out of us, and they always made out so you would think they were losing money hand over fist. They were just trying to squeeze us dry, which they're still trying to do.

GRIFFIN: But that specific thing, the album cover, that wasn't over money, was it?

JAGGER: No, but later on, I discovered how much money they'd made, and we'd made nothing. I'm not in the business just to make money, but it does put you a bit uptight. Plus the fact that they were just downright uncooperative, which I think is bad with an artist. But this is like the old-fashioned English way of dealing with artists. They're just a piece of old thing that you just kick around. They're not there to be looked after, unless they're opera stars. And if you don't behave like opera stars, you don't get treated like opera stars. That's one thing I have learned. Which is terribly draggy, to have to perform like that. But if you just be nice, then they just kick you up your proverbial.

GRIFFIN: **Did you find it difficult at the time to decide who to do the licence with?**

JAGGER: The licensing deal was a difficult decision. We had no money. We thought we'd worked hard. We'd been successful, but we didn't have any money. We just didn't have any money. We talked to everyone, but we didn't take the deal with the most money. We just took the one with the people we liked best.

GRIFFIN: **How much did the personal charm and persuasion of Ahmet Ertegun at Atlantic have to do with it?**

JAGGER: A lot really. I found Ahmet the easiest to deal with. He seemed to be a more or less permanent feature at Atlantic. Not all people in record companies are permanently there. He was a pretty understanding person. We have disagreements, but we have good times too.

GRIFFIN: **Still on the business side, how much longer are you going to have to live outside the country?**

JAGGER: As long as I want to, really. I like to come to England, probably more than anywhere. But I like it here [in the States] as well. I was in a position where if I didn't leave the country, I would be in a terrible mess. I don't mean broke, which I don't mind being. I mean more than broke — that means owing. So I had to get out of the country, to pay the tax that had been incurred for me. That's why I had to leave. Simple.

GRIFFIN: **Moving on to the drugs period, how resentful did you feel at the time in 1967 when, the whole year, you were constantly being harassed both by the law and by the popular press?**

JAGGER: It's really difficult to put into perspective, because I'm still being harassed. Like when no one else is, you know. They were really nasty and mean. They just were mean — all that handcuffs, you know, on four pep pill charges. It's just daft when I think about it. It was just so absurd. They tried to blow it up, which is what they try to do, to make it some kind of thing. That's the way they work, that's the way the establishment works, particularly the police. I'm not saying the judges. But the police, they really make it more than it ever is. And it's got to be big — they don't think they've got anything going unless they've got the kitchen sink

★

thrown in. I mean, the evidence they didn't use was hair-raising. They didn't even dare use it themselves. They even overstepped the mark . . . I'm not going to tell you what it was, I'm probably breaking some law by even speaking about it, I don't know.

GRIFFIN: You mentioned the establishment, but it was strange that the very pillar of the establishment, *The Times*, came out with a leader article in your defence. How did that *Times* leader affect you?

30 JUNE, 1967, MICK AND KEITH ARE RELEASED ON BAIL AFTER DRUGS CHARGES.
'THEY WERE REALLY NASTY AND MEAN,' SAYS MICK

JAGGER: It affected me greatly. I was in jail, and somebody threw it through the window, which is illegal in jail. It was very nice. That was what sort of got me out, or helped us get off, or whatever. It was against normal press conduct, and that shows a strong sense of purpose. It was something I'll always remember, and be grateful for, which got me out of that mess.

GRIFFIN: You yourself seem to have come through it intact. What can you assess as the effect that it had on Brian [Jones]?

JAGGER: He wasn't immediately involved in that particular one that I was in, but yes, it ruined him. People can get ruined by that harassment, by police. The same guy that busted Brian was the one that busted me in 1969. The second time it happened to Brian was too much. He just couldn't take it. He was too sensitive, you know. Or some people might say too weak. But he wasn't a criminal, he was a musician, you know. You've got to be tough to be a criminal. If you choose to be a criminal, and you're going to rob people and hit people over the head, you've got to be tough. You've got to take what's coming to you and all that. But this guy was just a musician, and he just wanted to get on with being a musician. And he was just being harassed, and his mind couldn't take it.

GRIFFIN: **Do you think, up until the time this happened to you, that a lot of people weren't aware that this had been standard practice among musicians for years?**

JAGGER: The general public doesn't know anything even now. Like people in Japan think I'm walking around with needles stuck out of my arms. They seriously believe it. They think I'm an incoherent, idiotic junkie. To me, I'm just an ordinary English bloke, same as everyone else.

GRIFFIN: **I know that you yourself are still suffering from some of this harassment.**

JAGGER: I am. I'm not allowed to come to America because of what they did to me in 1969. Unfortunately, I can't say on the BBC what did happen to me. But I'm still suffering from what I consider to have been unjust treatment.

GRIFFIN: **But the climate generally, especially in England, seems to be a lot easier now.**

JAGGER: It is in most places. But what I think about drugs . . . . Firstly, I don't think that anybody should go to prison for drugs, unless they're really making millions out of it, or are just making people's life a misery. I don't think people who take drugs should go to prison. I don't think that's going to have any effect on them whatsoever. I don't think that people should be stopped from moving from A to B, merely because they may have been convicted on some minor charge. It's very easy to get into America if you've hit an old lady over the head, but it's very difficult to get in if someone says you've smoked a joint. I also don't think that hard drugs are very good for anyone, because I don't think that most people can handle them. I just don't think that people can handle drugs, period. Most people can't. A lot of people can't handle alcohol. Most people are addicted to cigarettes. A lot of people are addicted to hard drugs. They just cannot handle them. They get ill, they rely on them, they fall to bits — it's horrible.

GRIFFIN: **What about the time of Brian leaving the group and Mick [Taylor] joining? How much effect did it have on the general direction of the group?**

JAGGER: A lot. Brian had a sort of indefinable thing. He had a lot of nice things going, always flitting around, always doing something, like flashes of really nice brilliant things. Then after that, we lost that kind of indefinable thing, and we had a kind of lead guitar player, so that changed the sound. Judge for yourself.

GRIFFIN: Looking back, ten years ago did you think you would ever become as big as you became, or that you'd still be doing this?

JAGGER: No, we never thought we would be anything. Certainly we never thought we'd go on as long as we have. Even if you read — what was it called? — *Fab* magazine in 1964, we all said, 'We'll do this for a couple of years', you know. And that's how we really felt. People would say, 'How long can you really go on doing this?' This was in 1964! We'd say, 'Well, a couple of years.' Then in 1966 they'd say the same. I don't know.

GRIFFIN: OK, I'll put the question to you now. How much longer do you think you'll go on now?

JAGGER: [LAUGHS] Not again. I don't know. I'd like to see some changes. Different music. But it does change, that's the thing. The music does change. What we were doing in 1967 is vastly different from what we're doing now. Even what we're doing this year is different from what we were doing last year, I think. You were at the studio last night — it doesn't sound the same, does it? I'm the one that always complains when I think it's all the same. But it's not really.

GRIFFIN: So it'll go on for a while yet, then?

JAGGER: I suppose so. We really don't plan very much ahead, we just keep going.

GRIFFIN: In most of your interviews, you always say you couldn't imagine getting married.

JAGGER: I can't imagine being married now, I'll tell you. [LAUGHS] It doesn't really feel any different. My old lady, I don't know what she'd say. She'd probably scream at me in Spanish or something, but I don't really think it's necessary. I still feel the same about it, so I just carry on the same, and I find that works. You might find that rather contradictory, but everyone's life's contradictory.

GRIFFIN: How did you feel in the days when almost weekly there would be articles in the paper about some headmaster who'd had a go at his kids, saying they were behaving like those bestial Rolling Stones?

JAGGER: I love all that. I thought that was a great period. That hasn't happened since. It hasn't happened to Marc Bolan, or David [Bowie], or no one. That was just a great period. It's never happened again — I don't see how it can.

KEITH RICHARDS

GRIFFIN: **How did you gain the confidence to be able to start writing and performing your own material?**

RICHARDS: Writing, I suppose really the credit for that must go to Andrew [Oldham, the Stones' manager], because I'd never thought of writing. It had never occurred to me. I though that was something else, like being a novelist or a computer operator. It was just a completely different field, that I hadn't thought of. I just thought of myself as a guitar player. It hadn't occurred to Mick either. Although I suppose we dabbled with it occasionally, when we were sitting around with Brian, but I remember we just gave up in despair. It was Andrew who really forced Mick and I to sit down and try it, and who got us through that initial period that you have to go through where you just write absolute rubbish. You just rewrite other people's songs. Until you start coming up with songs of your own. It was Andrew that made us persevere with that. Maybe because he wanted to promote the group, and get as much out of us as possible, I suppose.

GRIFFIN: **Has your approach to songwriting changed much over the years?**

RICHARDS: No, not really. When you're writing for somebody like the Stones, unless there's a conscious change, like there was in '67, when everyone wanted to do different things and try out things — unless there's a conscious effort, there's the same approach still. You write songs which you know the band are going to be really able to get their teeth into.

GRIFFIN: **How do you see yourself writing in the future? Can you imagine writing for people other than the Stones?**

RICHARDS: I can imagine it, yes. I can do it. I wouldn't think it would be that much of an effort to write for somebody else. It would just require the time that I put into the Stones. But it takes up most of the time, really, to write enough material, enough Stones fodder for a year. But if things change, I've no doubt I could write for — the Queen Mother if I had to.

GRIFFIN: **What about your playing? Have you changed your approach on that much during the years?**

RICHARDS: Yeah, that's changed a bit. I use a lot of different techniques now, compared to when I started. The main thing, just through listening to really good blues guitar players over the years, and going into it a lot more than I did then, I've got into a lot of different tunings and stuff. Mainly I did all this about '68, '69. I started fooling around with different tunings. I play on stage now for about half

KEITH – 'I FEEL WE'LL GO ON FOR A WHILE'

the show, and for half the songs I record, using a five-string guitar, tuned to open G, which gives a much different sound. For a rhythm guitar player, there's a lot more you can do with it, for rock 'n' roll and for blues. It's the tuning they used to use in the thirties, a lot of the old guitar players used open tuning. It gives a very full sound to the chord, because you've got no finger positions at all. You've got straight bar, and you can make other chords. You can make different combinations of chords than you can with straight concert tuning. You get a really full, thick sound.

GRIFFIN: **Are you influenced at all by modern guitarists?**

RICHARDS: Yes, Mick Taylor's influenced me an awful lot. Just playing with him has given me a lot of ideas. And I've been influenced by Clapton. There's never been anything he's done which hasn't knocked me out. Probably 75 per cent of all the guitar players in England go for being a soloist or a virtuoso, which burns a lot of people out. You can see a lot of them drop very young. But I've never been interested in knocking off the fastest, most exhilarating solo — the fastest gun in the West sort of attitude. It hasn't really been my hang-up.

GRIFFIN: **Which leads us on to playing on stage. A lot of bands have got to the point where they're so successful, they can just release one LP a year, maybe do a few topline venues and leave it at that. The Stones seem to have got out and worked, and gone to people. Is this because you really enjoy doing it?**

RICHARDS: Basically, it's because we enjoy it still. And the other thing is, there's no point in having a band if it doesn't get up there for a good portion of the time and play in front of people. That's what a band is all about. That's how they start off, by playing three or four hours every night. If you're lucky enough to be successful, and just lie back and record a minimum of tracks, and just do a few gigs, you're like a car engine, man, just kicking on four cylinders instead of eight. You're just not getting the full potential out of anybody. A band really needs those moments on stage when you're really cooking, just to keep you going. That gives you the inspiration for other things, to carry on.

GRIFFIN: **If it was easier to arrange, would you like to work even more than you do?**

RICHARDS: Yes. You see, with the Stones, it's difficult, because a tour takes months to line up now. Sure I'd like to be able to call up the guys one morning, and say 'Let's play tonight', because that's how it grabs you sometimes. But you can't do that. Setting up gigs these days is a big operation — security and all this shit.

GRIFFIN: **Drugs. How painful is it for you, looking back to 1967?**

MICK AND KEITH PERFORMING TOGETHER – 'A BAND REALLY NEEDS THOSE MOMENTS ON STAGE WHEN YOU'RE REALLY COOKING'

RICHARDS: It was a painful year. It was a big year. 1967 was a year of change for everybody. 1967 was the explosion of the drug culture, if there is such a thing. That's when it came into the open from underground. Everybody started talking about it. And throughout this whole year, we were having to put up with this incredible hassle, this confrontation with policemen and judges. I feel very uncomfortable looking at a uniform anyway, and having to deal with these people for a whole year really did wear us down a bit. In fact, it put us on our back really for eighteen months or so. It wasn't until we got into *Beggars Banquet* that the whole thing managed to slide into the past. Though at that time it was still bugging Brian like mad, and Mick. I suppose it was the fact that so many people, including the press, or sections of it, had been dying for so long to have a go at us. There are certain things which went on behind the scenes which are very unsavoury, and which once and for all destroyed my faith in the fairness and impartiality of the English judicial system. Only when you create a fuss and get it up to the highest level, then they start to reconsider.

GRIFFIN: **Can you be magnanimous now, and think that in a way you were bearing the cross for all your younger followers and for what was going on?**

RICHARDS: We carried a lot of things, being the focal point of a generation. But they've given us a lot of incredibly good times. Some fantastic experiences, and they are continuing to do so. Also from being in that position, I've learned that if it turns around on you, it turns round heavy. So you have to be prepared for that. That's probably the lesson I learned from 1967 and that whole thing.

GRIFFIN: **The other thing that you learned the hard way is how to have your business affairs handled properly. What are your views about that?**

RICHARDS: Rock 'n' roll is a big business, you know. Musicians who find themselves suddenly the focal point of millions and millions of dollars neither have the time nor the inclination to be able to look after it all properly. You do need somebody to do it. Unfortunately, the record business, like a lot of other businesses, is run by a lot of very sharp people. There again, the thing I've learned, and it's a very simple answer, is that with anything involving bread, the only real way to deal with it is to take anything that's offered to you and give it to an independent lawyer, and let them look it over. It's a very simple answer, but it's taken us a long time to learn it. I'd be the Maharajah of God Knows Where if I'd had all the money that we'd have earned. It's a very sore point, because on top of the things that you've been through, to see good friends and people still being led by the same — how can I put it? — still being involved with what we know to be a very dodgy situation, and to see it still going on, when we'd hoped that, knowing what we've been through, people would be a little more wary. The whole area of rock 'n' roll business and politics is a very, very tough game. If you get into it, you find that you've no time for anything else. So the best thing to do is what we did, which was to ignore it as much as possible, and just hope for the best. That's really what it comes down to, you just hope for the best and learn what you can along the road to protect your own interests. That's all you can do. You can never possibly learn the whole thing and still be a musician. So rock 'n' roll musicians always get the bad end of the deal.

GRIFFIN: **Can you remember how hard it was in the early days?**

RICHARDS: Oh yes, it's ingrained in me. Between Mick, Brian and myself, we were pretty determined. There was no other way for it to go except up. Since we were determined that we were going to stick together and play, and since we were down to thieving potatoes out of supermarkets anyway, and selling beer bottles back to the off-licence, there was nothing else to do except push on. It had to get better, even if it didn't get fantastic. It was difficult, but it was fun too. We were only nineteen or something. We didn't give a shit anyway.

GRIFFIN: **But how did you cope with it then, because the rise was really. . . .**

RICHARDS: Meteoric, yes. Everybody went through their star trip. I think Brian was the only one that it changed in a really deep way, and probably not for the better. He couldn't cope with it, really. It did change him almost immediately. Immediately, he started getting disillusioned. It was very difficult for him, not made any easier, probably, by the rest of us, because nobody had the time to look after somebody else. You've got your own trips you're going through. On top of that, you're working every night. If you're not working, you're recording. When that's going on for two or three years non-stop, it's all you can do just to keep yourself

★

going. To look after another cat as well, it's impossible. That's one of the sadder things about stardom. And when it happens that fast, especially if you're in with a group of people, if one of them isn't quite strong enough to deal with that situation, there's very little you can do to help him.

GRIFFIN: **Do you think therefore that the parting of the ways was inevitable?**

RICHARDS: Eventually, yes. It did take a long time. It took from '63 to '69 for it to come about. I don't know what Brian would have gone on to do, quite honestly. Even though he was talking about getting a new band together and doing it all again, I don't think that that's what he would have ended up doing if he had lived. I think he might have gone into movie music, or maybe something entirely different, collecting butterflies or something. But I don't think he was leaving the Stones just to start it all over again with some other band.

GRIFFIN: **How shocked were you when you actually heard that he'd died?**

RICHARDS: It was a complete shock. I always knew Brian was a very fragile person. When I think about it, there are certain people you meet — and Brian was probably one of them — who you couldn't imagine getting old. He's one of those people that you know are going to go fairly young, because they burn it all up so quick. Nevertheless, that didn't lessen the shock when it happened. Being with that cat for seven or eight years non-stop, you know, to have him suddenly removed completely, it really knocked us back.

GRIFFIN: **That gig that you did at Hyde Park only three days later must have been really difficult, not only for you, but also for Mick Taylor on his first appearance.**

RICHARDS: There was just a feeling amongst us that we just had to get on with it, and the best way was just to do it as soon as possible, and show everybody that the rest of us were still alive and kicking. That's probably the best thing we could have done.

GRIFFIN: **How far do you think Mick Taylor's joining the group has changed the musical direction?**

RICHARDS: It's difficult to say. The band is still improving, it's still getting better. I still feel there's more to come from it, and probably a lot of that's due to Mick. A bit of new blood in there is always a good thing. He contributes a lot, in the studio, in the construction of records, he's getting to know a lot more about recording now, something he hasn't done a lot of until this point. He's OK.

GRIFFIN: **Looking back on your whole career, did you think that you'd ever be as big, and that you'd go on as long as this?**

★

RICHARDS: It's funny. You always know it. Mick and I talked about it a lot. I knew it from the minute I first heard Elvis that that's what I wanted to do. Once you've decided that you want to be the best rock 'n' roller in the world, you go ahead and try it. Would I have seen it going on this long? No. That was one of the things that worried me when it all started to happen, you know, Stones-mania, and all that period. Up to that time, nobody had a life expectancy of more than two or three years. Apart from Elvis. So I was worried that it was all going to be over within a couple of years, when I was only just starting to learn it and dig it. But things have changed since then, and as far as I can see now we can carry on doing what we want to do and let it grow and let it mature and so on for quite a while. So I'm quite hopeful that as long as I want to do it, I can do it. If we want to stop, we can, but I don't see any diminished enthusiasm from anybody, so I feel we'll go on for a while.

KEITH RICHARDS ON STAGE IN '73 – 'THE BAND IS STILL IMPROVING'

THE ROLLING STONES ★ 1973

SINGLES	REACHED
Angie	UK No. 5
Angie	US No. 1

ALBUMS	REACHED
More Hot Rocks (Compilation)	US No. 9
Goat's Head Soup	UK No. 1
Goat's Head Soup	US No. 1

1974

CARL WILSON

THE BEACH BOYS STORY was a series of six programmes in 1974, produced by Jeff Griffin. The interviews were carried out by Radio 1's Bob Harris.

'I'm an enormous fan of The Beach Boys, but pulling together the interviews for The Beach Boys Story was one of the most difficult projects I've ever been involved with, simply because of the way the band worked at the time. Really, they were in total disarray, and if it hadn't been for Carl, I doubt if we'd have managed to pin the rest of the band down at all.

'After The Beatles conquered America in the early sixties, The Beach Boys had come under enormous pressure to match their success, to be the Apple Pie answer to the Fab Four. Brian Wilson as the creative genius of the group had particularly felt that pressure, and by the time we came to do the programme, he was well into the five-year period he spent 'in his room', where really he just locked himself away from the world with only his music. Carl had assumed leadership of the band, but when we followed them as they prepared for a gig in Colorado Springs, it became clear that they hadn't really got it together. Only Carl rehearsed properly with the session musicians they had taken on, the others just drifted in and out as they pleased. Later, on stage, they had clearly lost the magical chemistry that had made them so great. But somehow the family ties between them kept them together, and eventually Brian re-emerged and they got it together again on stage. Carl's answers to my questions in the interview disguise a very difficult time in the group's history.'

HARRIS: Can we start at the very beginning, Carl, and talk about the way that the band came together?

WILSON: The first thing I seem to remember is Dennis [Wilson] and Michael [Love] going to the beach one day a long time ago, and they came back and were talking about making a song, about surfing and going to the beach. This was in the Fall of '61. That's the first thing I remember, as far as the reality of a group goes. But before that we'd always, you know, got round a piano to sing, and we'd go Christmas carolling, and we've always been into music somehow since childhood. We just said, 'Well, let's see, Dennis and Mike and Brian, and Carl', and Brian had a friend Al [Jardine], and that was it. It was really simple.

HARRIS: Let's talk about the early records. Did you try and get the atmosphere of the surfing feeling on records? Did you expect that kind of feeling to communicate itself in the way that it did in those early days?

WILSON: I think in the very beginning we were just making records, you know, just recording. It was very innocent. We didn't know — we just sang and tried to record. And then it became more of a musical thing for us, after we learned and started to grow musically. Then we started to make an effort, making good music, and trying to make a good sound.

THE EARLY BEACH BOYS, CARL SEATED WITH GUITAR
– 'IN THE VERY BEGINNING, IT WAS ALL VERY
INNOCENT'

HARRIS: Did you think of it as kind of local music at the time?

WILSON: It was most definitely local, for sure.

HARRIS: Were you surprised by the response in other parts of the country and outside America? Did you think they would understand the feeling in the music outside this area?

WILSON: That's it. It was the feeling in the music, more than what the lyrics were saying. The feeling was good. Music is a great thing, and we were mostly interested in the sound, and the feeling that the sound creates. It was really a great thing for us to have people enjoy it. It was a way-out experience, because, you know, we didn't know. We just sang and recorded.

HARRIS: Can we talk a bit about Brian's decision to stop touring. What actually led up to his decision?

WILSON: He never did like touring, ever. He didn't like flying, or being away from home or anything. So I think it was just a thing that was bound to happen. He just said 'I don't want to tour, I want to stay home. I want to make good music.' I remember my dad was upset about that. He thought it wasn't fair for him not to go and play for the people because they'd bought the records, and they wanted to see him. Anyway, he just said he wouldn't do it because he wanted to write. I remember it was in Houston. He really got upset, and he just had to leave. I think that's one of what people call his nervous breakdowns, but it wasn't really — it was just that he was holding it in and it just came out. He just said, 'No, I can't do it, and I'm stopping', and that was it. There was a thing where it hurt his ears, you know. He can only hear in his left ear, so I think all the high sound-pressure level was just too much. And he's more creative, so just doing the same thing every night over a given tour . . . he's just very sensitive, you know. That was the last gig he did, in Houston, Texas. It sort of frightened us, to think that he wouldn't be travelling, but we just went on and it was cool. I think Glen Campbell did some gigs with us for a couple of months, then Bruce [Johnston] joined the group shortly after that.

HARRIS: Coming on to *Pet Sounds*, had you deliberately tried things out on previous albums leading up to *Pet Sounds*?

WILSON: Brian would just get an idea, and that would be it. As for the songs, they came out very spontaneously, as far as writing melodies and making up tunes. It was like it was almost automatic. We made up some really nice songs. 'God Only Knows', I think, came out in five minutes. It came right through.

HARRIS: How did people respond to the album?

WILSON: Capital Records were a little bit afraid of it, because they probably thought they'd lose a market or a segment of people. They said, 'Give us some bubblegum music, because that's your great thing and we can get on the charts with that.' Anyway, for us, [*Pet Sounds*] was the best we could do at the time, and we thought it was good for us, so it just happened. They [Capitol] were very resistant to going forward musically. We were really angry with them. Brian just couldn't understand how they couldn't be into it. We just sensed that we wanted to improve, wanted to make good music. Up until that time it was mostly singles. He wanted to make albums. That was really before albums became a thing. I think it really took the Beatles for people to get hold of the idea that you could buy albums and that was a great form of entertainment.

HARRIS: **Did you record 'Good Vibrations' as part of the *Pet Sounds* sessions?**

WILSON: It was all at the same time. Brian called me up and played this weird thing on the phone, and it was 'Good Vibrations'. It was a really funky track. It had more of a 'let it rip' drums, smashing and stuff, then it sort of refined itself.

HARRIS: **The response to 'Good Vibrations' and to *Pet Sounds* was absolutely incredible. But that was immediately followed by a period which was really your worst period in terms of people's response to what you were doing.**

BEACH BOY
CARL WILSON

WILSON: I would agree. We did quite a lot of change up to that time. But it just was too much. You can only take so much. So we just cooled it. It was trying to break a whole pattern of the business control and the whole thing. But the sessions started to loosen up quite a lot by then. They started to be very loose, and sometimes we didn't record at all. We just would sort of rehearse, or we'd do

something else. I think the pressure was a little much for Brian then, because I think whereas the direction had been really strong, straight ahead, you know, it started to waver and become unsure. So we just needed the time to rest and get out of that. So it was a real freaky time, it really was.

HARRIS: **We should talk about your own writing and your involvement in production.**

WILSON: *Surf's Up* was when it really, for writing, for me . . . I write a lot of stuff now, but just during the time we started to do *Surf's Up* was when we started to do some more gigs, and the group started to really become active at that time. And I started to write, too. I just got inspired and started to write.

HARRIS: **Your involvement with transcendental meditation, what was the start of that?**

WILSON: We did a UNICEF benefit in Paris in December of 1967, and the Maharishi [Mahesh Yogi] was there coincidentally to set up a centre, and so we just met. I believe he came to see Ravi Shankar at the rehearsal, and I met him there. Dennis came back in the dressing room and said, 'The Maharishi is in the audience', so I went right out and sat next to him. We started talking, and we went to his hotel and talked for hours and hours. Then the next day, we all got initiated. It's been of benefit, it's been of great benefit, because it's been wild, it really has been wild, at times. I think meditation has really helped us cope with the different things, the pressures, you know, and just everything that's happened. Somehow, just a group of people coming together to make music can really cause a stir — it's really something. But music is great, just the idea of people making music is a stroke of great fortune. Just to be able to make music, and to make a living by it is very lucky.

HARRIS: **So, Holland. Can we talk about the reasons for the move there?**

WILSON: Well, we wanted a change. We were really fed up with what was happening at that time. That's when all the lawsuits and everything started to happen, and we just wanted a change. It was like, 'Well, why don't we do this?' and everybody said, 'Yeah'. Had we had time to think about it, I think maybe we would have decided against it, for practical reasons, because it was really an expensive move, on a business level. To spend that much money to make a record doesn't make sense from that standpoint. But we're not too practical when it comes to recording — in the economic sense. We never have been, really. The main thing is to be able to make a good sound. It seems ridiculous to me to try to make music and to think, 'Oh, well, we're going to have to not do this because of this.' It's absurd. The reality of it is that people can only stay in the studio so long, as long as their budget will permit, so we just got under all that by getting our own studio.

But it was well worth it, in the sense that going to a place like that makes it a one-purpose thing. To be in a completely new environment and to be there for a purpose gets through to the music. We got going in July, and it was very nice. It was really a group.

HARRIS: **And now, at the new studio you've built here in California, you've also been careful to make sure that things are right. There's a meditation room, and a room for the kids.**

WILSON: If we're going to spend a lot of time there — and I think we are, for the next couple of years anyway — it should be a really pleasant atmosphere. It should just have the things that make recording nice. Michael and Al both live away, so it's sort of a thing where they can come down and spend a few days, and really be comfy.

HARRIS: **It must be good to be back in the studio after so long. How is the new album coming along?**

WILSON: I think what we'll do now is just record, and then we'll see what direction we want to go in. It's not like we're trying to think of a concept, or trying to make a particular sound. We're going to record, and see how and what we're doing, and we'll take the direction from there. I think that's the most logical approach right now.

HARRIS: **How long are you expecting to take on this one?**

WILSON: As long as it takes. I don't think we're going to try to meet any schedule.

HARRIS: **What's Brian's day-to-day involvement with the band? Does he have the same degree of involvement now as you have, for example?**

WILSON: Not right now. We're getting ready to go away for the weekend, and he's not involved in that at all. But he has a way of getting a lot done without doing too much. It's really something. I wish I had that knack. It's just really strange. My friend was telling me about his chart, and in his chart he — I don't know what you call it — but he has, like, one opposition . . . I don't know, but that would seem right, because he really gets things done with less effort. But he's all over the records, all the cuts. And he's always helping with the arrangements. I was doing something on the track to 'Long Promised Road' — I think I was overdubbing something one evening — and he made up an arrangement just because he heard it through the wall. He said, 'I made up an arrangement. I couldn't help it. I heard it so many times, I just started humming along with this arrangement.'

BRIAN WILSON IN THE STUDIO – 'HE HAS A PARTICULAR GREATNESS,' SAYS CARL

HARRIS: How much recording has the band done with other people over the years?

WILSON: Not a lot. We sang on an Elton thing last week, Elton John. 'Don't Let the Sun Go Down on Me' – that's a nice tune. And Dennis and Alan and myself sang on a Chicago cut when we were playing in Denver in November. But that really is it.

HARRIS: Looking back over the last ten years or so, where would you place the Beach Boys? How important do you think their contribution has been?

40
★

W I L S O N :   It's very difficult to say. I think Brian's influence is massive, I really do. I think he showed people that you can make really fine music, and it just opened up, like a door flew open. But as far as the Beach Boys? They're just records. I think the Beach Boys made some good records. I think 'Good Vibrations' was a good record. I think in its point in time it was a really fine record, really different. But I think Brian's influence really goes a long way. He has a particular greatness.

THE BEACH BOYS ★ 1974	
SINGLES	**REACHED**
Surfin' USA (re-release)	US No. 36
ALBUMS	**REACHED**
Beach Boys in Concert	US No. 25
Endless Summer (compilation)	US No.1

MARC BOLAN

THE STORY OF POP was a major *Radio 1* series in *1974* which summarised the previous twenty-five years of popular music, year by year. A number of staff at Radio 1 contributed to it, and dozens of musicians, great and small, were interviewed. When Radio 1's John Pidgeon heard that Marc Bolan was in the building for another programme, he thought he would try to snatch a few words with him. After all, Bolan had surely done more than provide a few catchy hits. Like his friend David Bowie, he had crossed over from the 'alternative' scene, or 'underground', into enormous mainstream success and had proved an innovator in both music and image. Bolan had also been the first pop star to wear glitter — and now everyone was doing it. He was an eye-catching character, as John Pidgeon remembers:

'The trademark corkscrew curls looked a lot better on him than on his beefy minder, hired to protect him from the army of teenage fans — which I have to say was diminishing slightly by this time. In the end, very little of this interview was actually included in the finished programme, even though it revealed Marc to be a very charming and interesting man. It was the time when the glitter movement was just taking off, and one of the highlights for me looking back is when Marc describes how he set the whole ball rolling by casually wiping a smear of his wife's glitter under each eye before a photo session, only to find the look adopted immediately by his audience.'

PIDGEON: **When you first started making music, you were part of what was known then as the 'underground'.**

BOLAN: The thing about the so-called underground in those days was that there was basically nowhere for anyone to play, which is the most important point. I started playing in Hyde Park in 1967 and stood on street corners to get some bread to pay the fare home and back. John Peel had just joined Radio 1 and did *Top Gear* and we got on that because I'd met John when he was in the pirates [radio stations]. Then a place called the Middle Earth — in fact it was called the Electric Garden then, if I remember correctly — opened and I went down there and they offered John an evening to play. We were going to play for nothing to about four people. He did it regularly for a couple of weeks and we always did it with him. I think we did about twenty minutes or something — never got paid of course — until suddenly there were about 2000 people coming in every week and we were one of the main groups there. I'm just trying to think who the other groups were — there was Tomorrow, Fairport Convention and Pink Floyd. Eventually we'd get about ten quid a night or something and then we started doing colleges and the whole thing grew out of that. But really there was nowhere else to play. It was a slight rebellion against what was happening in music at the time.

PIDGEON: **Well, yours was a rebellion because you were playing acoustic music, which had never really been thought of in terms of pop music. . . .**

BOLAN: Yes, obviously it changed later with the emergence of Cat Stevens and James Taylor, these kind of people, but the only other group similar to us at the time was the String Band who in fact — it was quite sneaky really — were much bigger than we were and I used to say 'Don't compare me to The Incredible String Band.' Of course everyone was going to and, once I'd said it, everyone did, so people thought of us as being as big as them, which we weren't.

PIDGEON: **How did the change come about? Was it just because, as you say, suddenly you found there were 2000 people turning up, or was there a desire on your part to make it in some other way?**

BOLAN: I never thought about success at all. I just thought about earning a living, just doing something and getting my songs heard by people. I never took it beyond that, but in that summer of peace and love — as someone once said — one wasn't ambitious. Everything seemed very nice and very funky and like it was going to last a long time, and secure, in a funny kind of crazy way, and friendly, which doesn't seem to really apply now somehow. There was a definite feel then that one shouldn't really worry about anything, a definite feel. Suddenly what would happen was people would come down to record us and I would turn most of them down.

MARC BOLAN – INTERVIEWED IN 1974

One day Tony Visconti came down who was working with the Move and Procol Harum and I said, 'I'll only sign with you if we can do an album' because it was more important for me to do an album than anything else. We couldn't get on television, we couldn't get any exposure at all, really. I remember the first day they only pressed 700 records and they sold them all in the first five minutes. Everyone was astounded and I thought 'Wow! 700,' but that was the naivety that one had then. Whereas now they can do 100 000 and you don't bat an eyelid, then 700 people going into a shop. . . .

PIDGEON: **Presumably those 700 people bought the record without any kind of promotion?**

BOLAN: Sure. There were obviously people who went to the clubs, because we were playing around a lot. And probably from [John Peel's] *Top Gear*, I would say that helped incredibly, us in particular. People like Captain Beefheart it helped and certainly Pink Floyd, because in the live sessions you could really do anything you wanted. It was a very interesting period. A lot of bands came out during that period. The Nice were another group.

But we were considered much more so — you know, a spearhead of this new thing which didn't even exist because all they were doing was making records which, you know, everyone wanted to do. The Floyd at the time did have a single in the charts. I wanted hits. I also wanted to make LPs. I did in fact stop putting singles out for two and a half years because I just felt it was less important than the LPs. Like a lot of people during that period I was into words and there was a lot of good pop music being made then by people like The Who and The Move who were also good writers. When I got into the T. Rex thing there were very few people making good singles. Hendrix would only make one over a long period. The Beatles, The Stones — it was one a year or something. So that was when I figured I ought to make some singles. I like singles. I've got a three-minute adrenalin buzz and singles are nice, they're interesting but they're not all-important, all-consuming, even to me they're still not. The albums are still much more important.

PIDGEON: **You said the fact that you were having hit albums meant that you weren't really underground any more by then. . . .**

BOLAN: It was a total illusion. It wasn't real because the groups that really were so-called underground couldn't get heard because all they were playing was Pink Floyd and Fleetwood Mac, or whatever. The thing about most underground groups at that time was they weren't very good, whereas later you began to learn how to play your instrument quite well and you got successful. But by then the whole thing had kind of petered out. It wasn't exciting any more. But don't forget, people like Hendrix came along and all those things changed it all around, which was very

★

beautiful actually. When Jimi put singles out and they were hits it all changed round. There was a definite change-round when that happened, whereas all the people initially involved at that time became successful and there was really nobody to follow them. A lot of people came out of that era if you look back on it now.

PIDGEON: **When did musicianship become important to you?**

BOLAN: I suppose in about '68. The first album I used as a vehicle for the songs. The second album was just a sound. I had a kind of guitar sound in my head but once we got to *Unicorn* I think I was really beginning to consider guitar playing, structures of songs and using other instruments. I played organ a bit. I goofed around. I mean I've only in the last three years taken guitar playing very seriously.

PIDGEON: **When did you first play electric?**

BOLAN: I started out playing electric with John's Children, another so-called underground group at the time. I wrote a song called 'Desdemona' and I played guitar on that. It was the only thing I could play then. I played quite well actually but that was the only song I could play on, literally. I just thought, 'Well, come on you can't just do one number for 25 minutes.' It's been known, mind you!

PIDGEON: **So, after rejecting the original idea of playing electric and going through your acoustic stage . . .**

BOLAN: Yeah, because I was just into songwriting, purely. I wasn't really concerned with technique or anything — just getting down lyrics, you know.

PIDGEON: **The words were obviously important. . . .**

BOLAN: Yes, they were much more important to me then, probably because I couldn't play very well.

PIDGEON: **The sort of ideas that you were writing in your lyrics, they were the sort of ideas that had come up with the underground?**

BOLAN: Yes, definitely. I think the reason why Tyrannosaurus Rex initially happened so fast in terms of that was because I was just reflecting and talking about things that most people thought or wanted to hear about at the time. It fitted the mood of the period, and the reason I stopped and got into the electric thing afterwards was because I felt that I'd done all I could within that realm. I had to change because I felt I would have gone sadly — no detriment to them — the same way as The Incredible String Band went, which was a slow drive into nowhere, really. You're just getting hung up on the same riff all the time.

PIDGEON: **But do you think that by coming back to the sort of mainstream of rock that you were . . .?**

BOLAN: It's finding a niche in the mainstream of rock, this is the thing, because it did change, as I say. I mean the emergence of Hendrix and Cream and all those people did make it possible to be respectable as well as selling a lot of product. As well as selling a lot of records you could still be a respected artist, which wasn't possible before. No one took The Who seriously until that period of time, and then it gained a new status.

PIDGEON: **So it wasn't just an owning up that the underground thing had not really had any lasting validity?**

BOLAN: I think one began to know that anyway, but I never thought about it like that. I don't think anyone did. You never do when you're actually part of it and it's happening. In retrospect, possibly one could think about it like that because it was, as I say, a mood, a feeling, but it certainly was not a religion or a way of life or anything like that. I mean they were the only interesting things that were happening. That's the point. It was interesting and it was a kind of raw excitement, untamed youth. It was kind of somewhere to be, something to belong to. Like Dylan was very important in that period of time because he was the only guy saying something sensible.

PIDGEON: **So how, specifically, did the change come about, the second change? From Tyrannosaurus Rex to T. Rex, from electric to acoustic?**

BOLAN: It was a slow thing because after I split with Steve Took I got Mickey [Finn], and *Beard of Stars*, the album we did, that was the last of Tyrannosaurus Rex — I played electric guitar on that — it just sort of came into it. I wanted to go higher on the scale than I could play on acoustic guitar. I'd also met Eric Clapton around that time, so I'd got to see other people and I saw Hendrix a lot. My background was basically rock 'n' roll, or heavier sounds if you want. People always used to think I was really into Indian music and all these things. I really wasn't. I had periods when I listened to that music, the occasional Ravi Shankar album, but I wasn't really into that at all. I used to burn incense though, I still do.

PIDGEON: **So which record was the turning point, in terms of appealing to a different kind of audience?**

BOLAN: For me that single or that album, *Beard of Stars*, because I could hear that I could probably get away from where I was, and almost sound like a rock 'n' roll band suddenly. When The Incredible String Band went so-called electric it just sounded like the String Band playing electrically, it was very quiet. Whereas I just went out and bought a Marshall 100 watt, plugged in and played loud, got my fuzzbox and my wah wah and got into that. Because I wasn't afraid of the guitar, I never have been. I'm a very aggressive player, so the second I got back into volume it was too exciting not to do it.

MARC ON STAGE – 'I'VE ALWAYS BEEN INTO A VISUAL THING BECAUSE I ENJOY IT'

PIDGEON: **So when in fact did the screaming girls start?**

BOLAN: 'Ride a White Swan' time. In fact 'Ride a White Swan' was taken from a science fiction story called 'Children of Rah', which is very heavy on that level. 'White Swan' I took out of that, and that was at the end of 1970.

PIDGEON: **So that in fact was just an electric treatment of the similar sort of things you'd been doing?**

BOLAN: Exactly the same, no difference at all. There are no drums on that. It was just the right time, that's all, for whatever that new feeling was and corkscrew hair. It was lucky, very lucky, I think.

PIDGEON: **You bring up corkscrew hair, so obviously the image had. . . .**

BOLAN: It must have something to do with it. It wasn't intentional, of course. I've had corkscrew hair all my life. I tried to straighten it once. But I think that because we got on television, *Top of the Pops*, with the single ['Ride a White Swan'] and the second we did that it went from Twenty to Number Two or something like that in two days — sold 300 000 in two days. Amazing. I was stunned because I was going to stop playing. I was going to go back to being a wandering poet.

PIDGEON: **But at that point you must have become very conscious of your image?**

BOLAN: No. I never have been. I've never changed. I look the same. If you've checked, looked through the albums, the first album cover, even though it was a painting, looked the same and was the same image.

PIDGEON: **Yes, but until that moment you just thought that was the way you looked, but then you must have realised it must make a difference?**

BOLAN: Well, I've always been into a visual thing because I enjoy it, but I never gave it much thought and I still don't particularly. I realise that people could relate to it and imitate it or whatever, but to me it was still the music. I never considered I'd be a teen idol or something and then when it actually happened I had to deal with it. But it still didn't affect the way I approached the music at all apart from the fact that there was a demand for more records and I'd gotten out of doing that. I found it exciting at the time. I was able to grow. It made me grow quicker than it would have done if I was in the environment I was in before.

PIDGEON: **When you first started playing on stage, how did the audiences change?**

BOLAN: The audiences very slowly changed, believe it or not, half-way through when 'White Swan' was a hit and we were doing the first ten-shilling tour, which was very underground. We were playing big halls to about three-quarters full and suddenly towards the end of the tour I realised something was changing. The kids were getting a bit younger and they were selling out the concerts, which they hadn't done before. And then I put out 'Hot Love' and it went straight to Number One and then all the audiences were much younger and predominantly chicks after my balls, which is very cute.

PIDGEON: **When you realised you could have this kind of effect did it make you complacent?**

BOLAN: No, when that kind of success hits you like that you don't think that much about it. Everything happens too fast to really sit back and think, 'Wow, now I'm a star, now I'm successful.' You just think, 'I've got to get that album finished' or, 'I've got to do that gig.' So much to do, so little time — that's all that happens to you, because you never get a chance to really lie back and think about it anyway. And when you do, it's too late normally to even worry about it.

PIDGEON: **Was there any pressure on you to repeat a formula that was obviously successful?**

BOLAN: Yes, but I put the pressure on myself, almost. You see if you can work within a three-minute format, which basically records are, it's very hard not to fall into a kind of structure which was basically led by the early rock writers, early Drifters records and all those things, and early Beatles records, of two verses, a middle eight, then two verses and finish. I've always been very good at writing a hook, which is fortunate. But I tried not to do that, tried very consciously, that's why I made 'Hot Love' so long, you know. I wanted to break the pattern. The single which is a Marc Bolan single called 'Whatever Happened to the Teenage Dream' is five and a half minutes long and lyrically it is not controversial but it is very 'un' my image.

THE LAST PICTURE OF MARC, WITH HIS FRIEND DAVID BOWIE, IN THE SUMMER OF 1977

PIDGEON: Although the image, as far as you're concerned, was just a natural part of you, you must have become aware that as far as some other people were concerned, or certainly as far as the business was concerned, there was a shift very strongly towards image, almost for itself?

BOLAN: Yeah, yeah. I think there still is. It's still happening. I kind of abandoned the idea of that. It becomes too boring, you see. I don't like to see pictures of myself stuck all over walls, particularly. I'm not as into that as a lot of people are. I don't structure things necessarily that way. I try and let them happen naturally and if I happen to look good that day, we'll take pictures and if I don't, then we won't. I'm sensible in that respect but it's never a conscious effort to say, 'I must look different for this photograph.' Like even that glitter thing – I mean what happened is my wife had some glitter, so I just put it on my fingers and stuck it under my eyes. It looked cute. I only ever wore it about four times and everyone thinks I was born in it! Look what happened to the world after that. I put glitter under my eyes and I went to the next concert. It was about two days after doing the TV show and the audience was splattered with glitter, which was very sweet and kind of startling because I'd only done it as a joke. I didn't have it on that night so they were probably well upset. But I think it caused a change, especially with cosmetics, 'cause it meant that guys could go on stage and be sexy stars or whatever, being, not effeminate, but not necessarily having to have the Brut aftershave on or something super-masculine. You could use make-up and things to brighten the act, to make it more, not glamorous, but to enhance the showmanship of the thing. I think it's got a bit crazy lately. But I don't wear make-up at all particularly, not even on stage any more, because I find it boring now. Once you do something and it's funky, people do it who wouldn't normally do it, like groups who would just be like The Shadows five years ago and then suddenly decide they've got to, I don't know, wear car wheels around their heads because it's trendy and it might sell records. You know next week they'd also wear Indian headdresses if everyone else had them on and they thought it would sell records, whereas I don't think any people of my period would do that. If they did it they'd do it because they wanted to.

MARC BOLAN AND T. REX ★ 1974	
SINGLES	**REACHED**
Teenage Dream	UK No. 13
Light of Love	UK No. 22
ALBUMS	**REACHED**
Zinc Alloy and the Hidden Riders of Tomorrow	UK No. 12

1975

PAUL SIMON

SIMON AND GARFUNKEL — TOGETHER AND ALONE *was the strange title of Stuart Grundy's 1975 portrait of the two men who had been the world's most successful musical double act. The duo had split up five years earlier.*

'The interviews with both Paul Simon and Art Garfunkel were recorded in December 1974 in Paul's manager's office,' recalls Stuart. 'It was around East 60th Street in New York. I like to think that actually getting Art to come into Paul's office for the interviews played some part in getting them back together to record 'My Little Town'. We had proposed doing a major series on Simon and Garfunkel, but Paul wanted to include their work as individuals. Hence the title of the series.

'Paul's a great genius, but he's difficult to talk to in an interview situation. He was also slightly worried about being involved with a series which was to sum up a career which he felt was far from over. He was familiar with the BBC from when he'd lived in the UK, and knew that if we were doing the series, it had to be absolutely correct, so he was very careful to get all the details right.

'I remember being very concerned about the level of background noise while we were recording — from sirens in the street and so on — but listening to the original tape again, at one point you can clearly hear 'Still Crazy' being played in the next room. What probably seemed like a nuisance at the time was to turn out to be one of his biggest solo hits.'

G R U N D Y : **Ever since the early days of Simon and Garfunkel, you've been generally regarded as a 'perfectionist' in the studio.**

S I M O N : I must say in defence of Simon and Garfunkel – people often called us 'perfectionists', but we were not looking for perfection. We were looking for some kind of magic in the music and sometimes it just took us a long time to find it, you know, but we were not out to make a perfect record. We just developed our ideas slowly and changed our minds a lot and had the opportunity to spend enormous quantities of studio time on our work because we were selling a sufficient amount of records, so that Columbia Records was reluctant to stop our patterns of work because they were successful.

PAUL SIMON, PERFORMING LIVE IN 1976

GRUNDY: But it could also be argued that you were really perhaps for the first time treating the business of making rock 'n' roll or pop music, or whatever you like to call it, as an art form. You were building up, as one would paint a picture.

SIMON: Well that's so. We were building up as you would paint a picture. I'll tell you another thing that counted. We were all so perfectly happy in the studio, *all* of us — me and Artie and [producer] Roy Halee — that I think we were content to spend plenty of time there. We sort of dragged our whole lives into the studio. People came to visit us in the studio, and we saw people and we ate in the studio. It was a very enjoyable way of passing our time. I think that that also contributed to the fact that we spent a lot of time there, because we were enjoying ourselves.

GRUNDY: And of course you've been able to continue that luxury, in a sense, by not only spending more time on making records but allowing more time perhaps between albums too, to get material together.

SIMON: Well it takes me a certain amount of time to write. I'm not very prolific. As soon as I have enough work to do, then I begin.

GRUNDY: When you say you're not very prolific, does that mean that you don't sit down and say: right, for the next two hours I'm going to write?

SIMON: Well I sometimes do that, but it doesn't necessarily mean that I end up with anything. Or I could end up with one line, or I could end up with something that I throw out. Just looking over the past, certainly I've produced less than ten songs a year initially. I think I've only written about seventy songs or so altogether since Simon and Garfunkel's *Wednesday Morning* album. Including everything, it's maybe seventy songs.

GRUNDY: What, do you mean to say that you've recorded and published *everything* that you've written, or have you thrown away quite a lot of material?

SIMON: There might be two or three songs, maybe, that I haven't done. I think every song that I've written, with the exception of one song, has been recorded. And that one song was supposed to be the twelfth song on the *Bridge Over Troubled Water* album. And we had such a big fight over it.

GRUNDY: What, you and Artie, you mean?

SIMON: Yeah. We had such a fight over this song. He didn't want to do it, and I wanted to do it. He wanted to do a Bach cantata. He wanted to do all the eight voices himself, and I didn't want to. And I wanted to do this song that I wrote called 'Cuba Si, Nixon No' and Artie didn't want to do it. I looked at it again about two years ago and in retrospect Artie may have been right.

GRUNDY: So you're talking obviously about differences or a difference. Had you tended to have a lot of differences in the studio or on the level at which you had to decide what you were going to wind up with?

SIMON: Well let me say that we had many more points of agreement than we had points of difference, but we did differ, and the bigger we got, the more insistent we got that each one of us should have his way. So it became more difficult to resolve points of difference, whereas in the earlier days we found compromises a bit easier.

GRUNDY: Most of the best partnerships – and obviously you did have for a long time a very successful partnership – most of the best partnerships result from complementary pieces that you add. Would it be possible for you to stand back from the two of you and say what you felt were your relative strengths and weaknesses?

SIMON: Artie always seemed to really like my songs, which made it easy to work with him. I always felt that they were good because he always told me that they were good, so it was a positive way to begin work. And the voices blended well, we'd been singing since we were thirteen so we really knew each other's voice. And we'd been friends for that long so we didn't have too many problems in compromising. It really wasn't until the differences in our tastes became more ingrained that the problems arose. Then we were both capable of being very stubborn people. So it worked for a long time and probably would have worked for a longer period of time had not the movies come in to . . . to add an additional strain to an already complex and strained relationship.

GRUNDY: So in a sense *The Graduate*, whilst it . . . .

SIMON: It wasn't *The Graduate*, it was *Catch 22*. [Filming for *Catch 22*, in which Garfunkel appeared, overran, which meant he could not attend the recording of parts of *Bridge Over Troubled Water*.]

I believe that it's inevitable that partnerships break up, particularly these kind of partnerships. And I believe that they would have broken up anyway. But perhaps later, maybe a year or two later. But maybe it's really lucky that it did break up. To break up with *Bridge Over Troubled Water* being our greatest success. It was a good way to end, rather than to have come up with another record that would have been, I'm sure, less successful than *Bridge Over Troubled Water*, and then break up and it's not really quite the same.

But it was weird, it was a weird partnership, I will say that. There was something, some kind of understanding that we had between us that really made it a good partnership when it was swinging. We understood each other very well, because

SIMON AND GARFUNKEL – 'THERE WAS SOME KIND OF UNDERSTANDING BETWEEN US THAT REALLY MADE IT
A GOOD PARTNERSHIP WHEN IT WAS SWINGING'

we knew each other for so long that we were able to talk in a virtual shorthand. And our senses of humour were the same — we just about taught each other our sense of humour in fact. So really that partnership had some really good days on a personal level, and they far outweighed the bad days at the end. That's my opinion. I'm sure that's Artie's opinion too. Although at the time I was really angry, I really was.

GRUNDY: **Can you look at your own songs and use the word 'affection' in relation to your own material?**

SIMON: Well some songs don't embarrass me, let me put it that way. That's about the best I can say to you.

GRUNDY: **Well most people who are in any creative area find it very difficult because they're hypercritical, they find it difficult to think that they've done a good job.**

SIMON: That's sort of me. I don't very often think I've done a good job. And I don't like the majority of what I do. I shouldn't say I don't like it, but I'm not satisfied with almost everything that I do. I don't consider myself to be a major talent and so the only solace I can take is to hope that I'm growing. So if I'm disappointed in what I do, I can rationalise it by saying, well I'll do it better some time in the future. It's pointless to be critical of your stuff once it's done, really. So I don't spend a lot of time going over it and agonising over it because once it's done, you just leave it and move on to whatever else you're doing. Even if you don't like it, it's of no importance once it's finished. You did it, you did your best and you walk on and that's it.

GRUNDY: **Is there anything that you haven't looked back on and said, 'I could have done that a hell of a lot better?'**

SIMON: Oh, there are things that I did as well as I was capable of doing and I feel pleased with them. There are several things that fall into that category. I think 'Bridge Over Troubled Water' was a very good song and I think Artie sang it beautifully. I think he did really a great, a very soulful job to come out of a white singer. He sang it white, but soulful, and that's very hard to hear today. And I think 'The Boxer' was a really nice record — I like to listen to that record. And I think 'American Tune' is a nice song. And I think I've written several . . . nice songs. But I don't think I've written any great songs.

GRUNDY: **The separation of you and Artie was, in a sense, a release and a new beginning because you were starting afresh.**

SIMON: Well that's an aspect of it, yes. It was dangerous again, to a certain degree, to go and start all over again as just me. I was nervous . . . it's good to be nervous. After all those years of automatic success, you don't get nervous any more. It's really necessary to be nervous and be a little bit frightened. You try to work at your best and be afraid that even if you don't really do it as well as you can, that people won't like it or they won't listen to you. It kind of pumps the adrenalin into you and you really get down there and try.

GRUNDY: **Has there ever been a situation where you felt there had been pressure, either from the record company or from fans?**

SIMON: No, the record company don't bother me at all. They stay out of my way and whenever the record is finished, they take it. And as for fans, I don't feel any pressure from fans. But I'm always in some kind of state of emotional turmoil or something. I mean, I would not describe myself as happy-go-lucky. I feel under a lot of pressure all the time. That's not to say that I'm not happy. However, a good case could be made . . . [LAUGHS] that I'm not.

GRUNDY: **Is this a pressure for you to continue to prove yourself?**

SIMON: I really couldn't explain it. I wish I knew. I've a song on a new album — in fact maybe I'll call the album it — called 'Still Crazy After All These Years'.

GRUNDY: **Now you're working on solo albums, I wonder if you could look at the different paths that you and Artie have taken musically since the split. In what way do you think you took off and then he took off? In what directions?**

SIMON: Well the main difference between us is that I was writing songs for Simon and Garfunkel and I'm [now] writing songs for me. It's hard for me to say. Both Roy and Artie liked things to be cleaner than I did, more precise, more lush, they liked ballads. I like ballads too, but Artie is a particularly fine ballad singer, a much better ballad singer than I am. So he really does tend to emphasise ballads. I try and mix up my stuff, ballads and up-tempos. And the rest comes down to simply a manifestation of our individual tastes, in him choosing what he wants to sing and in me choosing what I want to write, which of course I then sing.

GRUNDY: **It would be very easy for you to drop out of music altogether, actually.**

SIMON: I think it would be very difficult. Why do you say that?

GRUNDY: **Well, I would have thought that certainly financially you don't need to continue.**

SIMON: I'm not in it for the money. I like music. I love to write music. I love music. I don't think it's possible for me to . . . I can't imagine myself not playing or singing or writing. I would have to do something musical. It would just drive me crazy if I didn't.

'I CAN'T IMAGINE MYSELF NOT PLAYING OR SINGING OR WRITING'

PAUL SIMON ★ 1975

SINGLES	REACHED
Gone At Last	US No. 23
My Little Town	
(with Art Garfunkel)	US No. 9

ALBUMS	REACHED
Still Crazy After All These Years	US No. 1
Still Crazy After All These Years	UK No. 6

1976

DAVID BOWIE

DAVID BOWIE was a four-part series on the man who was undoubtedly the most creative, outrageous and colourful rock star in the five years leading up to 1976. Radio 1 presenter and producer Stuart Grundy had been fascinated by Bowie ever since their first meeting.

'It was in 1971,' he recalls. 'David came into the BBC in a lovely salmon-pink dress. By the time we did the series in 1976, his chameleon style was well established, with quite regular changes in his image as well as his musical style. The interviews were recorded in Berlin and Hamburg while he was on tour. His incarnation at the time was the Thin White Duke, so he was looking like a tea planter, with a beautiful pale suit, and orange slicked-back hair. He talked about himself in a very direct way, very objectively, also with a good deal of humour when he looked back on some of his previous images.

'I saw the Thin White Duke concerts in Hamburg, and Bowie was without doubt the only thing on stage worth looking at. He just glows on stage, with an incredibly magnetic personality. Face to face, he's a totally different person — there is magnetism, but he's not performing in the same way as on stage. He comes across as a very agreeable and funny person.'

BOWIE, THE THIN WHITE DUKE – 'HE WAS THE ONLY THING ON STAGE WORTH LOOKING AT,' RECALLS
INTERVIEWER STUART GRUNDY

GRUNDY: [NARRATING]   David Bowie has worn many masks in the ten years that he's been writing and recording, a fact that does set him apart from his contemporaries in the music business and makes one hesitate before using words such as 'singer' or even 'pop star' to describe him. In this series, I'll be looking at some of the faces and phases of David Bowie. It's plain to see, at this distance anyway, that Bowie was never just a pop singer. Pop music was providing him with a means of expression, expression that needed some sort of outlet.

BOWIE: I never really knew if I wanted to be a short-story writer. A singer really was the last thing I wanted to be. I knew I wanted to write words, in some kind of either poem form or prose. I wrote them as little stories and it seemed quite easy to set them to music. So they became songs. I guess if I hadn't had any sort of musical inspiration of any kind, I would have been a writer, a straight writer. I would have written novels, I think.

GRUNDY: Although he had the songs and ideas, Bowie required an arranger to put the dots down and a producer to put it all on tape. He found them in Paul Buckmaster and Gus Dudgeon.

BOWIE: I don't think I've ever produced an album like that first one which was called just *David Bowie*. I contributed an awful lot of the ideas. If I hear it, I know what I like, you know. Over the last couple of years, I've got quite technical and I actually know what things do. But up until, I think, probably *Diamond Dogs*, and including *Diamond Dogs*, I didn't have a clue what anything did on a board. But the sound concept was very much mine, all the time. The only one I've been puzzled with was *Space Oddity*, I think it was a conglomerate production between Gus, myself, and Paul Buckmaster, of course. I think Paul was a very important part of that period. He introduced me to a lot. He was the one that took me out of the story-writing thing and introduced me to sound and the visual aspects of song.

GRUNDY: The single, 'Space Oddity', was not a hit when it was originally released.

BOWIE: It got some airplay, as we say in the biz, but it didn't get any people buying me and I wasn't asked to perform. So I suppose in that respect it was a bit of a failure. But the idea of writing some sort of short stories, I think that was quite 'novel' at the time (excuse the pun). I was quite satisfied with the way things were going. I hadn't found any voice style and I hadn't found any way to perform. I was sort of very much in the Tony Newley thing.

GRUNDY: If ever there was a hungry period, this was it. His interests flitted, sometimes soared from one thing to another. He worked with mime artist, Lindsay Kemp, and they went into partnership with Hermione Farthingale.

B O W I E :   I was in a mixed media [LAUGHS] . . . a mixed media group – which means that one of us could dance, another one could sing and another one had some rotten poetry and we [LAUGHS] put it all together and went underground. It was called Feathers and the girl was Hermione Farthingale, who I fell in love with – and I'm glad I fell in love, because it gave rise to a lot of songs – and the guy was Hutch [John Hutchinson] on guitar . . . I don't know what Hutch is doing any more. And it was fairly successful. It was very influenced by Lindsay Kemp and the mime company. Most of the time it was earning a few pennies at the Roundhouse. It was fun.

G R U N D Y :   **Then later that same year, 1969, 'Space Oddity' was chosen as the theme to BBC Television's coverage of the moon landings, and went on to become a Top Ten hit. But what should have been an opportunity to really make a mark was frittered away. Bowie's discipline waned. He was shooting off in all directions, miming, meditating, making music, trying not to miss a moment.**

B O W I E :   Well, all this wild hectic experience [LAUGHS] was squeezed into only two or three years. 1971 is when I got down to serious writing and trying to not diversify too much. I mean, I was just diversifying all over the place. I would try and get involved in anything that I felt was a useful tool for an artistic medium, from writing songs to putting on art shows and street theatre. I was trying to be a one-man revolution. [LAUGHS]

G R U N D Y :   **While in the process of gathering together his first real band, Bowie gave them a trial outing on John Peel's Radio 1 show, *Top Gear*. As Bowie remembers, it wasn't all that good.**

B O W I E :   We rehearsed in the morning and did the show very badly. Then a couple of weeks later, we started working as a band called Hype and we did the Roundhouse. Oh, we bombed at the Roundhouse. Marc Bolan was the only person that clapped. We were all wearing Dan Dare outfits, I think, and Superman stuff. [LAUGHS] I don't know what we were doing there, we were right out of place.

G R U N D Y :   **Bowie was no nearer to finding any real success. He continued to get involved in pursuits that led to dead ends. His fickleness, though, was to make some sort of sense eventually.**

B O W I E :   Really it's an integral part of what I do now, but it's honed itself a little. It's more sophisticated, I guess, and a bit more mature. But I've still got that same erratic sort of faddy thing about me. I'll get turned on by something for only a couple of weeks and then I drop it a couple of weeks later. I went crazy over Man Ray photographs at one time, black-and-white photographs, and that lasted about a month. For me, it was the only thing, and I started taking Man Ray pictures – and then I changed my mind. I always supported myself with a reason why I changed my mind, but now I've realised that I just change my mind a lot. I'm just by nature a very flighty person. I get turned on and off things all the time very quickly and, having accepted that, it's a lot easier to live with it. I'm not going to have interest, a sustained interest in things — except with people. There's people that mean a lot to me.

GRUNDY: **Bowie was going through a lengthy phase of re-evaluation during those years. Was he coming to any conclusions, though?**

BOWIE: I thought, 'Well, here I am. I'm a bit mixed up creatively, I've got all these things going on. I'm not sure if I'm a mime or a songwriter or a singer or do I want to go back to painting again? Why am I doing any of these things?' Anyway, I realised that it was because I wanted to be well known [LAUGHS], basically. And that I wanted to be thought of as somebody who was very much a trendy person, rather than a trend. I didn't want to be a trend, I wanted to be the instigator of new ideas. I wanted to turn people on to new things and new perspectives. I always wanted to be that sort of catalytic kind of thing. I just decided to use the easiest medium to start off with, as rock 'n' roll is, and then add bits and pieces to it over the years. So that really by the end of it, I would be my own medium. I mean that'll happen hopefully one day. That's why I do it all . . . to become a medium.

GRUNDY: **The album *Man Who Sold the World* was written and recorded piecemeal with Bowie doing a lyric here, a music line there, with guitarist Mick Ronson and Tony Visconti arranging and recording as they went along.**

BOWIE: It was a nightmare, that album. I hated the actual process of making it. I'd never done an album with that kind of professionalism and that scared me a lot. I felt invalid somehow. I wished I were doing it on four-track at the time. We were on eight tracks and it all seemed too glossy. And also the subject matter was very telling for me. It was all family problems and analogies put into science fiction form.

GRUNDY: **But he had a surprise up his voluminous sleeve. When the album came out, its cover back and front featured him long-haired and wearing — a dress.**

BOWIE: Well that was a stab at being Pre-Raphaelite. [LAUGHS] That was my Gabriel Rossetti look. But it wasn't worth telling anybody that, so I said it was drag.

GRUNDY: **But there was even more controversy lined up to coincide with his next album, *Hunky Dory*. Two or three weeks after the release of the album, he casually mentioned to a pop press reporter that he was bisexual, always had been. Needless to say, it earned him huge headlines.**

BOWIE: Yeah . . . oh yeah, that went down very well, didn't it? [LAUGHS] It was a bit of a throwaway but I stuck to my guns. I think actually the one thing about that statement was at least it was a tag that people could sort of identify. It gave me a category, anyway. So I suppose it helped in that respect. When I got to America it meant a lot more. I mean it was a much heavier statement over there. It became radical and very political in a way, because they were going through the gay lib thing at the time. For the first couple of years I had a heavy battle because it was hard to tell people that although the whole bisexuality thing was part of me, it wasn't necessarily part of the work I did, and that because I wore funny clothes on stage, it didn't mean that I was into drag. But Americans don't appreciate the subtleties of dress as they do in Europe. In Europe, if you wear some funny clothes then it's seen as being part of the character you're playing. But in America, especially at that time, if you wore anything that wasn't jeans, it was drag. That was the hardest problem I had in the States, trying to convince people that because I was bisexual that it didn't mean that everything I wrote about or did was all gay. That the bisexual thing was part of my private life and none of their business. The songs and the albums and the stage performances were what I was all about, but the biggest obstacle I had was getting away from being put up there as some kind of token gay performer.

GRUNDY: **Back in 1972 it was the gay tag that he was trying, at least in part, to shed that accelerated him into adopting another role. One that he'd created and defined.**

BOWIE: I wanted to be anybody but me. I was wondering whether I would try and be me, or if I couldn't cope with that, then make up some people and would I be them easier? And that's how Ziggy got started, because I thought if I don't like being David Jones then we'll think up somebody else to be for a bit, and we came up with Ziggy. And it was much easier to be someone else, it worked better. So therefore I must have been an actor, I thought. Well, I'll be an actor, I'll say I'm an actor and that gives me a reason for changing and so I said I was an actor and then [LAUGHS] I came out with all these different guises. Now [in 1976] I seem to be finding it much easier to get nearer some kind of me. But I wonder, maybe I'm still acting up there.

GRUNDY: **Within six months of his *Hunky Dory* album coming out, David Bowie had another album following hot on the heels of a hit single. The single was 'Starman' and the new album, *The Rise and Fall of Ziggy Stardust* [*and the Spiders from Mars*]. Bowie's imagination, once sidetracked, had now homed in on a successful trail. Ziggy Stardust, the ultimate, the archetypal rock 'n' roller was perfect skin for the 'actor' Bowie to take refuge under.**

BOWIE: That's where the thing about poseur comes from. In English rock 'n' roll, it's the artist's stance. In America they really are rock 'n' rollers — they come straight out of factories and play guitars. But in England, you just tamper around with rock 'n' roll. You use it as something and I guess I was one of the first to really come out and say I'm using rock 'n' roll, that it's not my life, like it is to an American rock 'n' roller. Rock 'n' roll is quite fun and everything, but I'm only using it as a medium. And I think that's the typical attitude of the English rock 'n' roller, but I actually voiced it. I don't think it had been really voiced before then, that rock 'n' roll is used by the English.

GRUNDY: **Ziggy, of course, performed with his own band.**

BOWIE: It was Ziggy Stardust and the Spiders from Mars, and somehow or other, along the line, the Spiders got attached to David Bowie. So then the confusion set in about who was Ziggy and who was David Bowie. Even I didn't quite understand how all that happened. Suddenly I had a band called the Spiders, but I was willing to go with it because it worked on stage and I liked the ambiguity of not being quite able to set the personas, much like Nick Roeg's film, *The Man Who Fell to Earth*. It's the ominous enigma of split personality and which side is which, and having half the creation, the Spiders, who were just a figment of the imagination, actually working with a real character, David Bowie , on stage. That poses a serious head problem. And they played the part perfectly. I mean, I actually picked them for that. At the time, they were the number-one spacey punk rock band, they were absolutely archetypes, all of them.

GRUNDY: **Returning to the David/Ziggy question, it's interesting to speculate just how much of Bowie went on stage.**

BOWIE: There's no comparison between David Bowie on stage and David Bowie off. They're hopelessly different. It's a good release valve, a safety valve for me. I'm quite a cold emotionless figure on stage, but there's always that little last saving grace somewhere. I don't know what it is. If there's a nagging fear that one's not being accepted, I become sort of vaudevillian and then I'm back to this sort of shop-dummy mannequin thing again.

GRUNDY: **Was he living out his fantasies on stage?**

BOWIE: Well on stage, I don't like the idea of living at all. I can't stand the concept. You can't go on stage and live — it's absolutely false all the way and that's what I like about it. I can't stand the premise of going on in jeans and being real — that's impossible. There's not one man that can actually believe that he's giving them life, going out there with a pair of jeans on and a guitar and looking as real as he can be in front of 18000 people. I mean, it's not normal.

BOWIE AT THE LAST ZIGGY CONCERT IN 1973 – 'ZIGGY STARDUST WAS MY STATEMENT'

G R U N D Y : By the time that the 1973 American tour was over, Ziggy had outgrown his skin and another face was about to take over, the brightly flashed Aladdin Sane. And that meant the end for the Spiders.

B O W I E : It was because they weren't writing the stuff. They just knew that they were in a band called the Spiders and there was this thing that I'd written called *Ziggy Stardust and the Spiders*. So they were sort of playing the part. But for them they really were the Spiders. It must have been very anticlimactic when I said, 'Well, that show's all over now, you know. You can call yourself the Spiders, but really that's all done, because now I'm Aladdin Sane.'

Aladdin Sane was Ziggy Stardust meets *Fame*. *Ziggy Stardust* the album was an objective point-of-view album, and Aladdin Sane was himself talking about being a star and hitting America. I'd had that first experience of America so I had plenty of material for it. So it was a subjective Ziggy talking, really.

GRUNDY: **Advance sales for the *Aladdin Sane* album were over 100 000. It became a Number One album in Britain. But that theme again — insanity.**

BOWIE: Yeah, that's been part of the family, really. Well my family's nuts, vaguely, they're all pretty crazy . . . I don't know if they still are, I've not seen any of them for years. There's quite an amount of insanity within any family, I think. I think we've just got more than our share. But it's better to recognise the angels and devils within oneself. I think that prevents true insanity. I mean, I'm no more insane than the next man. But I keep making myself aware of how flighty I am and what a grasshopper I am and how my moods change such a lot, so drastically, and even my persona privately changes a lot 'cause one minute I can be quite verbose and articulate and the next minute I feel like a stumbling philistine. I can't even think the same way and my points of view change all the time. I think as long as you keep recognising it, you stand outside whoever's taken over at the time and the other one stands outside and has a look.

GRUNDY: **It's perhaps interesting at this point to look a little closer at how Bowie's creative juices flow.**

BOWIE: I spend most of the time just thinking about the concept and shape and size and texture of a thing, rather than the actual writing of it. But I think this is as important a part of creative work as actually doing anything like putting it down on paper or on tape. I spend quite a lot of time thinking — that tires me out and then I have a sleep, then I go and get drunk and I go and do things that I can think about the next day. [LAUGHS] And somewhere along the line they get transferred into actual physical matter, like an album or a photograph or a painting or something.

GRUNDY: **Anyway, on to *Diamond Dogs*, and the 1974 American tour that resulted from it.**

BOWIE: I started thinking about how hard it is for musicians to take part in rock theatre. That's when I tried to lose musicians on the *Diamond Dogs* show and that failed dismally because [LAUGHS] everybody complained. They said, [LAUGHS] 'We don't like playing behind these bleedin' screens.' [LAUGHS] I said, 'Well you've got to, because I haven't got any parts for you. But I don't want people to see you playing because it doesn't look like a street if there's a bass amp stuck in the middle.' [LAUGHS] But it was very hard to convince them about that. So they all left me. [LAUGHS] The show gradually fell apart — which it should have done because it was about a decaying city, so it was quite apropos that it should fall down in the middle of the tour. But everything really did start falling, it really did become a Diamond Dog sort of city.

G R U N D Y : Bowie's first major screen part was to come. Filmed in New Mexico last summer, Nicolas Roeg's film *The Man Who Fell to Earth* features Bowie as a visitor from another planet.

B O W I E : The film was the first thing that I'd been given where I didn't have to play a rock 'n' roll star, for a start. I wasn't required to sing. The only thing they asked me to do was to write some music, which I got out of doing because I didn't want my music to be attached to the film either. I didn't want it to sell on a soundtrack, I wanted it to be considered as a serious attempt at acting.

BOWIE AS *THE MAN WHO FELL TO EARTH* – 'FILM CREWS ARE VERY DIFFERENT
TO ROCK 'N' ROLL CREWS'

GRUNDY: **So how did Bowie's butterfly nature put up with the discipline of filming?**

BOWIE: The flitting that I do only comes in the creation of something. Once I settle down to it, I take the concept through to its logical conclusion. I don't fall out of love with things in the middle of them. If I'm serious about them, I'll do them. But once I've done them, I don't want to look at it any more or have anything to do with it.

GRUNDY: **There's a growing feeling among his friends and associates that perhaps David is beginning to lose his interest in music and is now recording and touring simply in order to finance his interest in films. He owns up to that last film being very much a means to an end.**

BOWIE: I want to work with directors that I admire just to see how they do it and why they got where they are. Artistically, how they arrive at their conclusions and to steal a little bit from each of them in technique and how to handle crews and things like that. Film crews are very different to rock 'n' roll crews. So I sit back and be very Capricorn and just sort of watch everything and learn how to do it, and then I'll go and do it better.

GRUNDY: **The Thin White Duke is the guise under which Bowie has been appearing on his most recent North American and European tours. He is, as you might imagine, quite critical of his own work, dismissing the greater part of it in a few words. What, then, was really worth while?**

BOWIE: The ones that I actually think are quite worthy of something were *Diamond Dogs* and *Ziggy Stardust*. *Ziggy Stardust*, I think is probably my definitive album, as I've been told. I'm very quick to own up that *Ziggy Stardust* was my statement. But I've always thought that you can only say one thing in rock 'n' roll, really, and everything else is just an expansion of that original statement. It certainly seems like that with the stuff that I've done. Some of it does qualify the original statement. This was my rock 'n' roll period. It dealt with this particular attitude, that rock 'n' roll is the decision of being establishment or non-establishment. That's the problem that rock 'n' roll poses — to be or not to be a rebel. That's what it says and always has said.

Diamond Dogs, though, is a very important album. I thought that was the nearest that I've done to a cinematic experience. For me, personally, it was my sort of Fritz Lang statement, it was my *Metropolis* in sound form. I think *Station to Station* is interesting. It's not important, but it's interesting because it seems to indicate some return to an earlier style of recording and writing for me. So I'm quite excited about the next one [*Low*]. I can't wait to see what it's going to be like. I expect it'll be quite interesting. I don't know if it'll be important, though. I think time tells that. It's always like painting to me, all of this, even the stage performance, the same. But recording especially, recording for me is just like doing a painting. You start off with a blank bit of canvas and you start work on it and sometimes it comes off, and sometimes it doesn't. There's no difference between that and painting. There really isn't.

DAVID BOWIE ★ 1976	
SINGLES	**REACHED**
Golden Years	UK No. 8
Golden Years	US No. 10
TVC 15	UK No. 33
ALBUMS	**REACHED**
Station to Station	UK No. 5
Station to Station	US No. 3
Changesonebowie (compilation)	UK No. 2
Changesonebowie	US No. 10

1977

FLEETWOOD MAC

FLEETWOOD MAC left the UK in the early seventies when they were still a blues band. While working in America, they had been beset by the kinds of problem that would have destroyed any other band. The creative leader, Peter Green, had left, a whole string of other band members had come and gone, they'd had legal difficulties and they'd even had to deal with a bogus 'Fleetwood Mac' touring under their name. But instead of breaking up, two of the band's core members, Mick Fleetwood and Christine McVie, strengthened the band through the creative input of the others. In early 1977, they returned to the UK to promote a new album called Rumours, as Radio 1 interviewer John Pidgeon recalls:

'I spoke to Mick and Christine in a suite at the Kensington Garden Hotel, overlooking Hyde Park. They had already had considerable success in the States, but not really here in the UK, so I remember asking Mick if he thought the new album, Rumours, would bring them the same success in the UK. His answer was a cautious, "I don't know". The next time I interviewed them was twelve years later for the Radio 1 series, Classic Albums, for which Rumours had been one of my first choices. Twenty-five million album sales in the intervening years had made a mockery of my original questions about Rumours, and about Fleetwood Mac's longevity, considering they'd been together a mere ten years in 1977.'

....

RUMOURS – IN EARLY '77, MICK FLEETWOOD WASN'T SURE WHETHER IT WOULD BE SUCCESSFUL

PIDGEON: By the time you get to 'Albatross', you're a long way away from the blues. That record certainly wouldn't have been that successful if it had only been bought by blues fans, would it?

FLEETWOOD: No, I think that was the record which upset a lot of people who'd been following the band. But it really didn't change the band instantly into something else. It was just something that came very naturally to Peter [Green]. It wasn't a thing where we said, 'Oh, I'm going to change what we're doing, I'm fed up with playing twelve-bar.' People, when they first heard it, were freaking out and saying we had gone down the drain. But really when they came to see us, we were still very much the same band, only that was in there as well. Obviously, we were all brought up with playing blues music, twelve-bar, night after night, so it didn't just disappear overnight.

PIDGEON: 'Albatross' got to Number One at the beginning of 1969, and it was actually an incredibly successful year for you in terms of the charts. There were two more singles that year. They were part of a development that began to make your music uncategorisable, other than to call it 'Fleetwood Mac music'.

FLEETWOOD: That's exactly how I answer now when people ask me, 'How do you put a name on it?' or, 'What are you doing now?' I think the answer is quite simply exactly what you've just said. There's no particular aspect that you can home in on and say, 'That's what Fleetwood Mac is.' And that was true then, and it's still true now. *Then Play On* as an album was when Fleetwood Mac ceased to be branded. I would say we played blues music prior to then. From *Then Play On* right through until now, the band is just a musical band.

PIDGEON: Particularly 'Oh, Well' and 'Green Manalishi' were quite extra-ordinary to hear for the first time. How did they come about?

FLEETWOOD: That's Peter Green — purely that. Obviously everyone else was playing on them, but it was very much his output in those tunes, and then — this is the drag — he stopped writing and stopped playing. It was just a scratching, probably, of what he could have been doing. But maybe not, maybe that was his final wad. Who knows? But they still hold up, both those songs. In the States, and especially 'Oh, Well', they've become almost like classics because of the fact that they do still hold up, which is a pleasant feeling for me.

PIDGEON: You were at a peak of popularity then, and it seemed a peak of creativity. But that was exactly the moment that Peter chose to quit the band, and quit the music business. It's impossible for an outsider to gauge the effect that losing a major creative force like his could have. What was it like?

FLEETWOOD: There was a floundering around within the band. Pete left on very responsible terms. We knew he was leaving, we were all psychologically prepared for it, and we all knew that the band wasn't going to break up. It would have been pretty horrific to lose someone who'd been responsible for a lot of the success of the band. Peter was very much the main force within Fleetwood Mac, creatively. Because of the warning, we all realised, Jeremy [Spencer], Danny [Kirwan] and John [McVie] and myself, that we didn't want to stop. But it was just a weird period, especially for Danny, who never particularly liked or enjoyed the stage side of it. He enjoyed writing or recording. John and I enjoy being on the road, but Danny didn't, and that was really the final reason why *he* left. In fact, I must be honest, Danny was asked to leave. That's the only person it has ever happened to. Everyone else just left in strange ways, you know. But that was the beginning of the strain, I think, on Danny: when Peter left and he was on his own. He was used to working and writing with Peter a lot. It was probably more of a trauma for him mentally.

PIDGEON: **In the light of Peter Green's departure, it's perhaps not surprising that *Kiln House*, the next album, should turn out to be quite a hotch-potch of styles.**

FLEETWOOD: That was mainly Jeremy's. Jeremy had done one solo album. All he'd done for us before was play piano on a couple of tracks on *Then Play On*. *Kiln House* was quite similar to his solo album where he did a lot of Buddy Holly

FLEETWOOD MAC BASKING IN THE GLORY OF A NUMBER ONE, 1969 (LEFT TO RIGHT) DANNY KIRWAN, MICK FLEETWOOD, JOHN McVIE, PETER GREEN AND JEREMY SPENCER

stuff, which I enjoyed doing. We all did. We spent a whole summer living together and rehearsing in a place called Kiln House, then we made the album. We didn't work in England. We went straight to America. I think we were all a bit scared to go out on the road here after Pete had left. And that was really the beginning of the demise in England. We pretty much ceased to work here. But luckily in America they took to the band, and we had a lot of good years touring over there.

PIDGEON: **Christine [McVie] took an unofficial part in the album, didn't she, and joined soon afterwards, which was just as well, because it was around that time that Jeremy left.**

FLEETWOOD: No, Jeremy was with the band for another eighteen months or so, with Christine. We toured with her extensively all over America, long three or four-month tours. We were just about to go on the road after finishing *Kiln House* and we were rehearsing. Christine was there, obviously, being married to John, and we suddenly all turned around and realised that the sound wasn't full enough for Jeremy to be able to get off on playing. He wanted a keyboard player, and Christine, with five days' warning, was a part of Fleetwood Mac. She knew all the numbers, she'd heard them day and night. And that was it. We left for America. She was in the band with Jeremy and Danny for about eighteen months, I think. Then Jeremy joined the Children of God and disappeared. And Peter flew out and saved our necks during an American tour. He finished the tour for us.

PIDGEON: **The fact that *Kiln House* did do something in the States must have helped restore your confidence, because presumably you were still recovering from the effects of Peter's departure.**

FLEETWOOD: Yes, it helped. But we definitely went downhill in Britain. We ceased to sell any records here at all up until very recently. We were selling 3 or 4000 copies of an album here, and that was definitely a big departure from what it had been at one point. But in America, that was the first album after Peter had left, and it set a precedent. We sold 200 to 250000 albums, and were able to work year in year out and keep the band going in America, and that's really where we stayed from that point until now.

PIDGEON: **Jeremy disappeared, and Peter helped out as a stopgap. Then you had to look round for a permanent replacement, and actually chose someone from California, Bob Welch.**

FLEETWOOD: He came from California, but he'd been living in France for three years. Through a mutual friend, we invited him over to meet us. That was the only time we'd ever auditioned anyone, before or since, for Fleetwood Mac. We had one day of auditions, which was horrific. We didn't know what on earth to do. Three or four people came down who had to play. But Bob was already living at our house then. He'd been there for, like, three or four days. So without actually playing with Bob, we got to know him really well as a person – he's really a great guy. No one else worked out, so we said, 'You're in.' Bob brought whatever he brought into the band – in England no one knows anything about the period with Bob Welch at all. In actual fact in America, prior to Stevie [Nicks] and Lindsey [Buckingham] joining, this was our most popular time, when Bob was in the band, i.e. Bob and Danny and Christine. That was the most noticeable period for albums like *Future Games* and *Bare Trees*, which all featured Bob. That was our peak, when the band definitely took off in a huge fashion.

PIDGEON: **Bob Welch's influence was immediately apparent on *Future Games*. The change in the music was quite distinct.**

McVIE: It was just a different guitar style and a different way of writing than we'd ever had in the band before. When you consider Peter and Jeremy and Danny, Bob Welch was definitely in a totally new direction, musically. He was also the first American in the band – very West Coast, very into jazz or jazz rock, jazz blues. It was definitely away from anything that the other three guitarists who'd been connected with us had done.

PIDGEON: **Danny Kirwan was the next to go in the Fleetwood Mac musical chairs. He was replaced by Bob Weston, and very briefly Dave Walker. The album, *Penguin*, which you did with both of them, sounds as if it was done by more than one band, it was such a mixture of styles.**

FLEETWOOD: Really, on *Penguin* the band was aware of the fact that although Dave was great on stage, as far as fitting into the character, it was a mistake. This isn't a reflection on Dave's work as a singer at all, it was just character-wise we made a mistake having a lead singer who wasn't musically involved in the band, who didn't really write any tunes. We found ourselves with a problem, and that's why even on *Penguin* Dave was featured very little. I think we were aware of the fact that we might have made a mistake. So we held back. Then, by the time we came round to making *Mystery to Me*, Bob and Christine were writing songs for Dave to sing. Then it got to the point where it just suddenly all hit us in one fell swoop that it wasn't going to work out, and we just had to say, 'Dave, it's no good.' So that was the end of that. Although *Mystery to Me* is quite a favourite album to me.

PIDGEON: **Then came the bogus Fleetwood Mac. How did that come about?**

FLEETWOOD: Well, it's a little bit delicate, because things in areas of court proceedings are still pending. But basically, what it came down to was our manager and ourselves had a huge falling-out over the fact that he was responsible for putting that band on the road. We didn't enjoy that experience one little bit. That was when the band ceased to work for about seven months, and we were all spending that time in lawyers' offices going backwards and forwards. It was a very negative time. It was a really traumatic experience for the band. It's the most threatening thing, when you've been involved in something for seven years, to have basically that taken away from you. Then, the main reason for recording *Heroes are Hard to Find*, the album which followed all that weirdness, was to get out of England. We'd had enough. It had been such a complete drag, I thought it would be a really positive thing to leave and go and record in Los Angeles, where Bob was living anyhow. We did that, and we've stayed there ever since.

PIDGEON: It was pretty impressive that you should come out of the other side of all those troubles, and make an album as good as *Heroes are Hard to Find*.

FLEETWOOD: In the States it had reasonable success, but nothing magnificent. I think that was probably one of the reasons, if not *the* reason, that Bob decided that he wanted to leave the band. He was very disappointed. We'd all worked incredibly hard to lead up to the point where we could even make an album, where we had it all sorted out and could go into a studio and record. We did *Heroes are Hard to Find*, and then we went out on the road. A lot of damage had been done by the bogus band touring, turning up and pretending they were Fleetwood Mac. The confidence had definitely been shaken in certain areas of America in the credibility of Fleetwood Mac. We worked incredibly hard over a four-month period on the road, trying to make good the situation, which we sort of did, but the album didn't really make it. It was just healthy, but nothing amazing. We were always lucky in America that we got a lot of airplay and always did, ever since we went over there in 1968. We've always been very well received by radio stations, luckily — which has probably had something to do with the survival. Anyhow, that wasn't enough for Bob. I think he felt complete disappointment, and really a little bit disillusioned with the whole thing, having worked incredibly hard, as well as being totally threatened by the situation that went down with the other band. So he decided to leave. And that's when Stevie and Lindsey joined, very shortly after that.

PIDGEON: And rather than damage the prospects of the band, Bob's departure brought about the most successful incarnation to date. How did the arrival of Lindsey and Stevie affect the band on stage?

McVIE: The whole visual side of the band changed radically with Stevie and Lindsey joining. We then seemed to become a very unified five members, with us all still happening to remain our individual selves, which is very interesting. I've never seen us, obviously, from out front, but I can imagine that it must be quite an interesting show to watch. And obviously musically, it's very versatile now. We haven't even started to explore the musical realms and musical possibilities amongst the five of us, the endless permutations.

PIDGEON: **Did anyone anticipate the phenomenal success of the album which was called simply *Fleetwood Mac*?**

FLEETWOOD: Not in terms of what it ended up doing, which is around four million copies. I think when we'd finished the album we felt within the band that it was a very different situation from four years before. We wanted very much for people to realise that it was a completely new band and how strongly we felt about the album that we'd made. So we as a band went out on the road before the album was even released, because we felt it was very important, having never played on stage together. We just did a fairly minimal amount of rehearsing really and we went out just so that we would feel comfortable, so that when the album came out we wouldn't be suffering from bad nerves going out on stage wondering what was going to happen. We went out for four or five weeks, and although all the halls weren't necessarily full, the audience reaction was incredible. They'd never heard or seen Stevie and Lindsey within Fleetwood Mac, and there was not one place where anybody thought, 'Where's Bob Welch?' It was completely the opposite. We felt completely confident being on stage. Let's face it, to a working band, which primarily we were, that's very important. The album came out and we were on the road for about four and half months fairly continuously, which again helped really push the album. It became over the course of a year a huge success.

McVIE: It pushed the album very gradually. It was one of those lingering albums. It took about eight months to reach its one and only week at Number One, but it has spent twelve to thirteen or fourteen months in the Top Twenty.

PIDGEON: **Do you think that *Rumours*, the new album, will do for you in this country what the last one did for you in the States?**

FLEETWOOD: I don't really know, but it's certainly noticeably doing well right now. That's very convenient for us, because when we arranged to come over and play here, we really hadn't got any success record-wise to speak of. People over here just knew that the band was doing well in America, and basically because the band are doing so incredibly well in America, it's taken this long to sort of come up the pipeline backwards, you know, and get over here.

PIDGEON: **Most bands when they start can only have a life expectancy of a few years, especially if you're talking about a period of sustained creativity. But you've been doing it for ten years now. What's the secret?**

McVIE: Versatility, I think.

FLEETWOOD: Also, I think anyone that's joined and come into Fleetwood Mac has never had that pressure of 'you've got to do this like so-and-so'. For instance, when Peter left the band, or Jeremy, or Danny, people have come in, and they have been totally free to come in with what they've got. Whether they're just a guitar player, or a writer, they've never had any pressure to write things in a certain way. That's really it. The reason they're in the band is because there's a lot of respect, otherwise they wouldn't be there to start with. The only thing is that you're working with four other people. To some degree obviously there's some compromise in that fact, but it's a healthy compromise. That's always how we've done things.

FLEETWOOD MAC ★ 1977	
SINGLES	**REACHED**
Go Your Own Way	US No. 10
Go Your Own Way	UK No. 38
Don't Stop	UK No. 32
Dreams	US No. 1
Dreams	UK No. 24
Don't Stop	US No. 3
You Make Loving Fun	US No. 9
ALBUMS	**REACHED**
Rumours	US No. 1
Rumours	made UK No. 1 in Jan 1978

RUMOURS SOLD TWENTY-FIVE MILLION COPIES WORLDWIDE FOR (LEFT TO RIGHT) JOHN McVIE, MICK FLEETWOOD, CHRISTINE McVIE, LINDSEY BUCKINGHAM AND STEVIE NICKS

1977

QUEEN

QUEEN was a two-part special in December 1977, presented by Tom Browne and produced by Paul Williams. Two years earlier, 'Bohemian Rhapsody' had transformed Queen from a cult rock band into mainstream stars. But there had been no compromise in the hard-edged approach to their music, and now as their following grew, they were also gaining a reputation as one of the best live acts around. But, as Tom Browne remembers, Queen as people turned out to be quite different from Queen on stage:

'Queen as people were not what I'd expected at all. There was no big star act, they weren't preoccupied with the traditional rock 'n' roll hang-ups. They were just four intelligent guys, professional musicians making music that the public were responding to. Freddie, of course, had this amazing flamboyant stage persona, but in the interview he turned out to be rather quiet and subdued. He took a back seat, and let the others have their say. I warmed to Roger Taylor immediately, and afterwards became quite friendly with him. Oddly enough, as I remember, John Deacon turned out to be the comedian of the group.'

BROWNE: Queen were formed in February 1971, and have become one of the most successful rock acts in the world, with six major albums and ten hit singles. Worldwide, Queen sales total over four million records. First of all, Freddie, how did it all begin?

MERCURY: Brian and Roger were in a very up-tempo raucous band called Smile, and I used to be in another band called Wreckage or something . . .

TAYLOR: Which was even more up-tempo.

MERCURY: And we used to be friends, you know, going to college together. We met up, and after a couple of years of knowing each other, we just decided we'd form a band together. It's as simple as that. We thought our musical ideas would blend. Then we met John, and decided to call the band Queen.

RADIO 1'S TOM BROWNE MEETS QUEEN IN DECEMBER 1977 – (LEFT TO RIGHT) ROGER TAYLOR, TOM, BRIAN MAY, (SEATED) JOHN DEACON AND FREDDIE MERCURY

BROWNE: **How long did it take you from the time that you'd made the demo to the time that you actually got a recording contract?**

TAYLOR: It felt like about eighty years. It was about eighteen months, two years.

BROWNE: **Was this style that you've created actually thought out from the outset, or did it just evolve as time went by?**

MAY: There were certain ideals that we had in our heads, definitely, certain patterns that we wanted to try and live up to. To put it crudely, I think we started off wanting to be a kind of heavy group, but with good melodies and with good harmonies. The other things grew out of that. The first album was really just putting down what we did on stage at the time. It was a quick 'into the studio' and a quick out. Even at that time, we had lots of big ideas about what we could do if we were let loose in the studio for a proper time. We saved all that up for *Queen II*. But a lot of the stuff for *Queen II* was written at the time we made the first album.

BROWNE: **John, you were playing bass, first of all.**

DEACON: Basically, I came down to London to university. I was here for about two years when I wasn't playing at all. I used to play before I came to university, in groups at school and things like that, but I gave it up when I came down. Then after I was here for about two years, I bumped into Roger and Brian somewhere. I heard just socially — because they happened to be at different colleges — that they were looking for a bass player. So I said I was interested, and went along for an audition. [TO THE OTHERS] I think you'd been together for about six months previously, hadn't you?

TAYLOR: As Queen, yes. We were going through about three bass players a week at the time, and we eventually found John.

BROWNE: **Did you immediately agree on the kind of music you wanted to play?**

DEACON: I don't know. They were already formed. They had all the musical ideas then of what they were trying to do, and I basically just knew I fitted in at that time.

MAY: He's very modest.

DEACON: Well, my development came later.

BROWNE: **You have a rather surrealistic approach — is that the right word — to your lyrics.**

MERCURY: I think an imaginative approach, yes. It really depends on what kind of song. I think at that time I was learning about a lot of things. About actual song structure. . . . As far as lyrics, they're very difficult for me. I find them quite a task. My strongest point is, say, melody content. I basically concentrate on that first, and song structure, and then the lyrics come afterwards.

BROWNE: **How do you sort out which songs are going to go onto an album, because you all write, don't you?**

DEACON: We row, argue.

MERCURY: We do write individually, so we go our separate ways when our tour is over, or whatever. Then we have a gleaning period, where we get together and play each other the new songs. Then what happens is a very huge sifting process, where we find out what songs go on the record — first, as far as the individual song is concerned, and also how the songs will sound with each other. So it's basically looking in terms of an album, as opposed to just individual songs.

TAYLOR: We have tried in the past to provide a lot of variety on each album, and a lot of contrasts, so we've had to have a good cross-section of material.

DEACON: *Queen II* is an album which in some ways is the root of all that happened thereafter. If people haven't heard that [music] before, you could hear it and think it's something off the new album, really. It still sounds that fresh to me. All the sort of textured work was there, the intricate harmonies, the guitar harmonies and stuff — the precursor of 'Bohemian Rhapsody' in many ways. It was also the first album which went into the charts.

MERCURY: Those were the days of sixteen-track studios. You have now twenty-four and thirty-two track. But we did so many overdubs on sixteen-track. We just kept piling it on and on and on, and the tape went transparent. It wouldn't take any more.

MAY: It went over the heads so many times with overdubbing, the oxide had worn off. It was a big step for us at the time, certainly. No one was really doing that kind of thing in those days.

TAYLOR: In fact, when this album came out, we were doing our first headlining tour. After supporting Mott the Hoople, and gaining an enormous amount of live experience, and a large following, really, for a relatively new band.

BROWNE: **You went on to support Mott the Hoople in the States, right?**

TAYLOR: Yes, it seemed a logical step, because it had worked so well, and we got on so well personally, which doesn't always happen on tours. So we really took the logical step and went to America with them as well. We did learn quite a lot from them. They're a really good live band. We had a very good American tour up to the point when Brian got hepatitis, and collapsed, and we had to come home. At which point things looked very black.

BROWNE: **Then you did an extraordinary thing. Having supported once in England, and having supported once in the States, you then went to headline straight away, first in England, then in the States.**

TAYLOR: It was quite rare then, because we did go in one step to playing the Rainbow by ourselves.

MERCURY: We take a lot of risks, actually. I think most of them have paid off.

BROWNE: **It's very obvious that you're a painstakingly thorough, very methodical group. You're perfectionists.**

TAYLOR: That sounds really boring.

BROWNE: **No, I think it's much to be admired, the fact that you go into every facet of production. Not only just the music – you see it right down to the last dot.**

DEACON: We always thought that was essential, not only in production, but in every detail we're involved in.

TAYLOR: We've learned through hard experience, really.

DEACON: Yes, right up to the last bit of print on the record cover, and the way it's cut on the album, which is crucial. Right down to the way the tours are set up. We try to keep control of everything. It's not easy.

DEACON: There's so much money involved these days. It's almost sordid to talk about the amounts of money, but they are involved, and people are very clever. Nothing corrupts like large sums of money. So we do have to be very careful.

BROWNE: **Brian, you in fact learned on a ukulele, from your father.**

MAY: That was the first instrument I played. My father had a genuine George Formby ukulele. George Formby was really the originator of that style of playing, which is rhythmic and melodic at the same time. He plays across the top and bottom strings to make little melodies. I'm really a pretty poor imitator of that style.

BROWNE: **I believe your father also helped make your first guitar.**

MAY: Yes, my father and I made my guitar together — which is still the one I use all the time. It was made out of lumps of wood, and bits and pieces. It cost about eight pounds to make.

BROWNE: **I read something about a fireplace.**

MAY: The hundred-year-old fireplace, the legendary fireplace! The neck was made out of an old fireplace, yes. We worked at it for a couple of years. I was at school, and it was evenings and weekends.

BROWNE: **And that's still the one you play now?**

MAY: Yes.

BROWNE: **Can we come to the colossal stage productions, with crowns appearing everywhere, thunderflashes all over the stage, you leaping about, Freddie, 'bringing ballet to the masses'.**

MERCURY: [LAUGHS] That's just meant to be taken tongue-in-cheek. It's just that at this point in time, that's something that interests me. I just try and incorporate it in the stage act. Nothing more, really. It's basically to enhance the music we play. If it wasn't working, then I wouldn't do it. And it's also a phase that I'm going through — and I like the Nijinsky costume!

TAYLOR: The people who come to the show seem to really enjoy them. Because you must aim for maximum effect, which we do, both aurally and visually. However, some people don't seem to like this, the so-called purists or whatever. They think it's 'techno-flash rock', but basically we're just trying to put over the music and the visual aspect, as effectively as we can, to as many people as we can.

MAY: The way we started off, we always had these big ideas, and we always thought it should be a visual and a sound experience. It should be a complete thing that you can wallow in, you know. I think it comes from when we were kids. If we wanted to see a rock band, we wanted to be knocked out, blown away. We think it should be a real event every time we play.

FREDDIE MERCURY – 'I LIKE THE NIJINSKY COSTUME – IT'S A PHASE I'M GOING THROUGH'

MERCURY: As far as we're concerned, we're putting on a show, it's not just another rendition of an album. If that was the case, we might as well just have cardboard cutouts, and just play the album through the system.

BROWNE: Do you find that the single helps to generate sales of an album?

TAYLOR: Definitely. That's what gets you to the mass of people. Even if they don't buy it, and even if they don't like it, they still know who you are from hearing the single. Whereas I think you could have a Number One album for six months, and people still wouldn't know who you were. But we never record any record as a single. It's always just a track off an album, that we think might make a good single after we've recorded it.

BROWNE: So you don't go into the studio and say, 'This is going to be the one.'

TAYLOR: No, never. We never have.

BROWNE: Do you take advice from other people as to what could be a single?

MAY: Never. It never works. Nobody wanted 'Bohemian Rhapsody' as a single, really. Everyone said no one would play it, because it was too long. Nobody except us wanted it.

MERCURY: But this is not to say that we're always right, because we're not. There's no sure-fire hit, there's no such thing. And with things like 'Bohemian Rhapsody', it was a big risk and it worked. With a song like that, it was either going to be a huge success, or a terrific flop. . . .

MAY: '. . . but it's been no bed of roses, no pleasure cruise . . .'.

BROWNE: 'Bohemian Rhapsody' was for me so amazing because it was such a departure from anything else that was in the charts in 1975. It stayed at Number One for nine weeks, didn't it? Freddie, can you tell a bit about how you recorded 'Bohemian Rhapsody', the actual technical side?

MERCURY: You want a few trade secrets? It was quite a mammoth task because it was basically done in three definite sections, and just pieced together. Each one required a lot of concentration. The opera section in the middle was the most taxing because we wanted to recreate a sort of huge operatic harmony section between just the three of us. That involved a lot of multitracking. I think between the three of us we recreated a 160 to 200-piece choir effect. . . . As we said before, we work on the album material and then we choose a single, and in the case of *A Night at the Opera* it happened to be 'Bohemian Rhapsody'. Then we made a film, which helped us a lot. A promotional film.

DEACON: We made the film in rather a short time, just before we went out to tour England. When 'Bohemian Rhapsody' was released, we were rehearsing up at Elstree. They just came in one night with a video truck, with their little bits, and we did it in about four hours.

TAYLOR: The film opened up a new avenue for us, because the film was used all round the world, and worked very successfully. It didn't only just get the record across. It got Queen across, both visually and aurally. That's really part of the accepted pattern of marketing a single for any major band, or in fact even a new band these days. They make the record, and bring out the record, but they always have the film with the record. In fact, you can send that film round the whole world, and literally promote your records with it, without actually being there. I think ABBA have turned that into great advantage.

BROWNE: **Finally, can we talk about Jimi Hendrix, because I know Jimi Hendrix has been a prime mover to the group, and a great influence to you all.**

FREDDIE – 'IN THE INTERVIEW, HE TURNED OUT TO BE RATHER QUIET AND SUBDUED'

MERCURY: He was just a beautiful man. I think he was a master showman, a dedicated musician . . . he was just everything as far as I was concerned. I went to numerous places to try and catch his shows. Just magic. It's quite a treat to watch somebody just come on stage . . . he didn't have the kind of props and things that we have today. It all emitted from *him*. It was just him and a guitar. Very colourful. It was quite a stage act. You learned a lot from that kind of thing.

QUEEN ★ 1977

SINGLES	REACHED
Somebody to Love	US No. 13
Tie Your Mother Down	UK No. 31
Queen's First EP/	
Good Old Fashioned Lover Boy	UK No. 17
We Are The Champions/	
We Will Rock You	UK No. 2

ALBUMS	REACHED
A Day At The Races	UK No. 1
A Day At The Races	US No. 5
News Of The World	UK No. 4
News Of The World	US No. 3

1977

JOHNNY ROTTEN

ROCK ON, *Radio 1's regular magazine show, could no longer ignore the Sex Pistols in November 1977. During the year, they had generated more press space than any band before them. While late-night DJ John Peel had supported the punk movement on air, bands like the Pistols had been largely snubbed by daytime programmes. But by the end of the year, developments suggested that the Sex Pistols were more than just hype. They signed a deal with WEA for American distribution, they went on the cover of Rolling Stone magazine, and on 12 November their compilation album Never Mind the Bollocks — Here's the Sex Pistols went straight to the top of the UK chart (displacing Cliff Richard's 40 Golden Greats). On 11 November Johnny Rotten was interviewed by Rock On's John Tobler, with Stuart Grundy producing. Their chat was pre-recorded because of fears of swearing, and the album's title was not mentioned on the programme.*

'I remember feeling very flattered when I found out this interview had popped up on a bootleg the following year,' remembers Tobler. 'The whole issue of bootlegs was very hot at the time, because an entire bootleg album of Pistols stuff had just come out to pre-empt Never Mind the Bollocks. They had found controversy at every turn, and although I'd interviewed a lot of the punks, I approached this one with a certain trepidation. However, Johnny Rotten turned out to be very straightforward — intelligent, but bitter about a lot of what had happened. He'd recently been attacked in the street, and I remember having to escort him to a waiting taxi afterwards.

'I still find their music brilliant. In early 1977, there was very little going on. There was just lots of overblown AOR American music. Although it made an enormous impact, a lot of punk music was more adrenalin than lasting value. The Pistols were different — they made some great rock 'n' roll records.'

TOBLER: Well, your album's come out. Once you said that you didn't think you were an album band. Does it really matter to you that you've had to put out an album which is basically a collection of singles with some other tracks, or do you really feel that it's an album?

ROTTEN: We didn't want the singles on it, or I didn't want the singles on it — I personally didn't — but the rest of the band didn't seem to mind. On this, we differed.

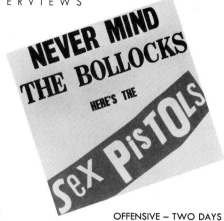

OFFENSIVE – TWO DAYS BEFORE ROTTEN'S CLASSIC INTERVIEW WAS RECORDED, POLICE TOOK ACTION TO STOP THE ALBUM BEING DISPLAYED IN SHOP WINDOWS

TOBLER: But it hasn't got the B-sides, which some people would think was pretty important. Do you think it's important?

ROTTEN: They were available as singles. If they wanted them then, they had a chance. If they miss them now, that's just too bad. There's nothing I can do about it. And I don't really care.

TOBLER: But particularly the B-side of 'Anarchy' – 'I Wanna Be Me' – that was only available somewhat briefly.

ROTTEN: To me, it's just an average dull song. I don't really care about it. In fact, I don't care about any of it. There's total disinterest.

TOBLER: Do you care about the bootleg?

ROTTEN: I don't like the idea of people making money out of me when it isn't me that's making the money out of them.

TOBLER: Is that a serious comment?

ROTTEN: Yes. I don't like people making money out of my efforts, when I'm not even given a look in. All that is material that we didn't want released, because to us it's sub-standard and should be kept unreleased at our discretion — not some git's. I don't like that. I think that's wrong, that's evil and nasty.

TOBLER: Do you know who did it?

ROTTEN: Yes. I'm not going to say, but I'll see him in court.

TOBLER: Are you in fact going to sue over it?

ROTTEN: How can you? How can you catch them? How can you prove it? We don't stand a hope in hell of winning anything in any court, not in this country, forget it.

T O B L E R : **The title of the album — whose decision was it?**

R O T T E N : Ours. Steve [Jones] always says it — that's his catchphrase. Because he's rude. And very fat.

T O B L E R : **And Sid Vicious' predecessor [Glen Matlock] . . .**

R O T T E N : Oh, fatty Tatlock . . .

T O B L E R : **. . . if you say so. Did he leave, or was he fired?**

R O T T E N : He was fired. I refused to have him in the band. I would have nothing to do with him. Everything about him was wrong. He was the man who wouldn't play 'God Save the Queen' on stage. Hated it. Didn't want anything to do with it. Hated '[Pretty] Vacant', hated 'Anarchy [In the UK]' and then coolly and calmly takes the credit for it in the press. That kind of rubbish annoys me. And that was just typical of him.

T O B L E R : **Did he in fact contribute a great deal to those songs?**

R O T T E N : He contributed as much as anybody else. It's a four-piece band, four members. No egos. That's why everybody gets credited the same, right? That's how it should be. He didn't actually like that, as I rightly remember. When it came to his way of thinking, he in fact wasn't credited on about 80 per cent of the songs. If the truth be known, then it should be known.

T O B L E R : **How do you think it got out, this rumour which has subsequently been denied, that there were session men playing on your original recordings?**

R O T T E N : That got out through total jealousy, and it's not even worth considering. I really don't care what people think. Does it matter?

T O B L E R : **Now, a question that's occurred to me is that Malcolm [McLaren], who I know you hold in great esteem . . .**

R O T T E N : That oaf!

T O B L E R : **. . . he was originally a Stones fan . . .**

ROTTEN: [LAUGHS] Typical. We went to his house in Clapham, and he's got this picture. It's meant to be a chair. Every time you go in there, he's trying to be all artistic and impress us, and we were laughing our heads off, thinking 'What an idiot'. And there's that Vivien [Westwood] squawking away in the corner, sewing things up.

T O B L E R : **In that case, why do you put up with them?**

R O T T E N : 'Cause we like them. They're our friends. Where would we be without Malkey-walkey?

10 MARCH 1977, THE SEX PISTOLS SIGN TO A&M RECORDS OUTSIDE BUCKINGHAM PALACE, WATCHED BY MANAGER, MALCOLM McLAREN – 'WHERE WOULD WE BE WITHOUT MALKEY-WALKEY?'

TOBLER: Anyway, he was a big Stones fan apparently, until he got terribly disappointed because they didn't blow the establishment like he thought they were going to. Do you think that the Sex Pistols was his way of trying to go the way that the Rolling Stones should have gone as far as he was concerned?

ROTTEN: I think he was a fool if he thought that about the Rolling Stones. Destroy the establishment? What the hell's the point? It destroys itself, it doesn't need help.

TOBLER: Has anybody ever said to you that Malcolm wanted to be what you are? To be the vocalist of the Sex Pistols?

ROTTEN: Yes, I read that as well. I don't know, and I don't care. I just know that I'm the best singer in the world. That's all I need to know. The most prolific, genius, poet of our times.

TOBLER: Your record hasn't quite come out in America yet, they haven't taken out the multi-million-dollar page ads all over the world for it yet.

ROTTEN: They're going to make us sound so gross. It'll be great. People will think we're pop stars riding around in limousines, and I really don't care what they think.

TOBLER: Do you want to go to America?

ROTTEN: Yeah, out of curiosity. I need a holiday. I mean what's this country done for us? What's the point? We can't play anywhere. Been banned all over the place. I mean, I don't see letters of complaint to the councils. I see nothing. They can buy their bits of plastic, great, but what's that?

TOBLER: But the fact that The Clash have been able to do some sort of tour indicates that somebody somewhere thinks it's getting easier, surely?

ROTTEN: It's because they don't really offer a threat of any kind.

TOBLER: Do you think any of the groups that came up at the same time as you have got anything worthwhile to say, or are any good?

ROTTEN: They didn't come up at the same time as us. They came up after. There's a subtle difference.

THE SEX PISTOLS ★ 1977	
SINGLES	**REACHED**
God Save the Queen	UK No. 2
Pretty Vacant	UK No. 6
Holidays In The Sun	UK No. 8
ALBUMS	**REACHED**
Never Mind The Bollocks — Here's The Sex Pistols	UK No. 1

JOHNNY ROTTEN AND SID VICIOUS LEAVE BRITAIN FOR THE US IN 1977 –

'WHAT'S THIS COUNTRY DONE FOR US?'

1977

ABBA

ABBA SPECIAL on *27 December 1977* was a one-hour programme based on two interviews with the group. DJ Tom Browne had spoken at length to the foursome the previous year, but in order to update the material, Radio 1 producer Paul Williams was dispatched to an international ABBA convention in Stockholm at the end of 1977.

It was the year when ABBA had been the world's bestselling band. They had had a total of six Number Ones in Britain, and their Greatest Hits and Arrival albums had been in the LP charts throughout the year. Worldwide ABBA sales totalled over fifty-five million records. It had been just three years since they rocketed to international fame after winning the 1974 Eurovision Song Contest with 'Waterloo'.

Tom Browne's interview formed the core of the programme:

'From the moment they walked in, ABBA were immediately impressive just as people. Even if they hadn't been pop stars, even if you'd just met them in the pub, you'd have been impressed. The girls, of course, were just stunning. Benny seemed to be the one who was in charge. Bjorn struck me as the more artistic, sensitive one.

'It was a time when the whole world was under the ABBA spell. On the day before the programme was broadcast, ABBA: The Movie had had its première in Stockholm. It was their first attempt at diversification. In the interviews they talk about further plans to extend their success into other areas, with business ventures like setting up their own studios, and creatively, by trying their hand at musicals. The sheer scale of the ABBA machine they describe — on tour, in business, in marketing around the world — reveals ABBA as the first, and greatest, of a new phenomenon: the global supergroup.'

DJ TOM BROWNE (SEATED) AND PRODUCER PAUL WILLIAMS MEET ABBA – 'FROM THE MOMENT THEY WALKED IN, THEY WERE IMMEDIATELY IMPRESSIVE'

BROWNE: It started, Benny, with the Hep Stars, right?

BENNY: For me it did, yes. Actually, it started much earlier than that, because my grandfather gave me an accordion when I was six years old. That's how I came into music.

BROWNE: Tell us about the Hep Stars. This was, what, 1962?

BENNY: Yes, that's when we started. It was about the same time when the Beatles were so popular all over the world. We did very well. We sold eight or nine gold records in Sweden. I think we outsold the Beatles.

BROWNE: Benny, then how did you meet Bjorn?

BENNY: Well, we met on the road actually. I was in The Hep Stars, and he was playing in a folk group, The Hootenanny Singers. And we just by coincidence met on the road the day before he was going to do his military service.

BROWNE: Did you do your military service, Bjorn?

BJORN: Certainly I did.

BROWNE: In The Hootenanny Singers, you were doing mostly traditional Swedish work, right?

BJORN: The group originated actually playing American folk music. But we went over to Swedish stuff because there was no group like that in Sweden at the time, and it seemed to be a good move.

BROWNE: **Then you came together with Benny and you made an album together.**

BENNY: Bjorn joined The Hep Stars for one season, and I joined the Hootenanny Singers for a summer, playing with them live on stage. And the more we worked together, the more the idea came forward of making an album together.

BJORN: Before that, we had written a lot of songs for other acts and other artists, which always did well.

BROWNE: **How about your career as a solo artist before this, Frida?**

FRIDA: I started at the age of thirteen, singing in a dance band. And so I went on for ten years in different dance bands. And one day I made a record, and so it started.

BROWNE: **Didn't it conflict with going to school, at thirteen?**

FRIDA: It was a big conflict, yes. Because I wanted to sing, you know, that was my life. But I didn't perform that much at that time, only once or twice a week.

BROWNE: **And what kind of dance band was it?**

FRIDA: It was a very old-fashioned dance band. Playing Swedish music, mixed with evergreens.

BROWNE: **Now, Agnetha, you also were a solo singer.**

AGNETHA: Yes, it started very early. I was just five years [old]. My father was working in the business. He was my manager. He did reviews. Then when I was fifteen, I started with a dance band, as Frida did.

BROWNE: **Then you made an LP, and you wrote all the songs on the LP.**

AGNETHA: Yes, I began to write my own songs when I was fifteen. I had a lot of success with that album in Sweden.

BROWNE: **Anna and Frida, how did you meet Bjorn and Benny?**

AGNETHA: By the time when Bjorn and Benny got together, Frida and I were working as solo artists. We had a lot of success. And Frida met Benny, and I met Bjorn. The first time I really got in touch with them I liked them very much, they were very nice.

BROWNE: Did they seem to have the same musical tastes? Were you aware of that when you first met them?

FRIDA: No, I didn't think about it at that time. We had other things to talk about!

BROWNE: On the first single which featured Benny and Bjorn together, 'Hey Old Man', I can hear the girls creeping in in the background.

BENNY: This was really the beginning of ABBA. Because we were together, engaged and all that, and had a social life together, they helped us out with the backing vocals. Because we're not two great singers, either of us.

BROWNE: Frida, you did a version of 'Fernando' in Swedish which was a big hit and went to Number One. How long was it at Number One?

FRIDA: We have a limit now in the Swedish chart, so they can't stay there more than ten weeks.

BROWNE: Tell us about the Swedish heat for the 1973 Eurovision Song Contest, where you came Number Three with 'Ring, Ring'.

FRIDA: We thought we had a good chance, but, you know, it was a so-called expert jury that time. If the people had chosen the melody to win, I think they would have chosen 'Ring, Ring'.

BROWNE: And how did it feel, going on to the stage?

FRIDA: Very tense. I remember Anna was pregnant at that time.

AGNETHA: Actually, I had gone one week over the time, so we were expecting the baby there.

....

LAUNCHPAD TO GLOBAL SUCCESS – ABBA AT EUROVISION 1974 – (LEFT TO RIGHT) BENNY, FRIDA, AGNETHA AND BJORN

BENNY: But it was actually lucky that we didn't win, because during that year up until 1974 we learned a lot about travelling and doing promotion and meeting people whom we were to work together with later on.

BROWNE: **One of the things I think is so clever is that you make videotapes of all your records, and you send them to different countries, so you don't actually have to go there physically. You can promote your stuff through the video medium. There's not many people doing this on the scale that you're doing it. How did this idea start?**

BJORN: Well, we realised that we couldn't go to Australia with every single. We couldn't even go to every country in Europe, so we started doing this, I think, back in 1975. It paid off very, very well.

BROWNE: **We've had many pop stars over here, such as Rod Stewart and the Stones, who have had to emigrate, because tax problems are just impossible in Britain. What's the situation in Sweden when you're making so much money? Are you paying an enormous amount of tax?**

BENNY: I think we pay maximum 87 per cent. That's maximum.

BROWNE: **Have you contemplated living in California or France or somewhere?**

BJORN: No, not really. Money isn't everything.

AGNETHA: And I think we love Sweden too much to move away from it.

BENNY: We've been playing around sometimes with the thought, like most people would, but when you travel as much as we do, you find very much that we're rooted, deeply rooted in Sweden.

BJORN: We try to solve the problem with taxes in another way. We don't take them out as a salary, we try to save them within the company, and invest them, and try to diversify.

BENNY: We can buy real estate, and things like that, just to make the money last over the period of ABBA.

BROWNE: **Bjorn, how did you react to the concert tour you did in February?**

BJORN: It was our first major concert tour, and our first time ever to appear in England. It took quite some time to get it on its feet. We travelled with . . . I think it was fifty people or so. A big band, to be able to recreate the sound.

B E N N Y : There are so many musicians on stage: three keyboard players, two guitar players, two drummers, three girls on back-up vocals. We have the musicians that we normally use in the studio.

B J O R N : But to prepare a tour, it takes too long, it's quite heavy. I think it'll take quite some time before we do it again.

[THE PROGRAMME NOW MOVES TO THE STOCKHOLM INTERVIEW]

B E N N Y : When we knew we were going on a concert tour, we thought we should have something a little apart from what everyone expected. And also for ourselves to get a kick to write for a more complete thing than just writing some new songs for the show. We came up with a sort of a story as a frame for a couple of songs. We've been talking about that for a long time now, doing a real musical. This was a sort of a trial to see what would come out of it.

ABBA – THE SUPERGROUP – IN 1977

WILLIAMS: These songs could form the framework of a stage musical, do you feel?

BJORN: No, not these particular songs. They are 'The Girl with the Golden Hair', as we call it.

WILLIAMS: Bjorn, I believe you're also building your own studio in Stockholm, which will be ready next summer.

BJORN: We're working on it, and we've seen the plans. It's going to be great. A really beautiful studio. Everything that is available, we will have there.

WILLIAMS: I've read that ABBA records are now being exported to Eastern bloc countries.

BJORN: We've sold some records to the Soviet Union, Poland, Czechoslovakia and so on. They pay less, but it's a nice feeling knowing that they listen to our music behind the Iron Curtain.

WILLIAMS: Can you tell us any other plans that you've got?

BENNY: We'll probably start writing again at the beginning of next year for another album or maybe, if we find an idea good enough, for a musical.

WILLIAMS: You don't particularly want to do a world tour or anything?

BENNY: Maybe, but not next year. Maybe the end of next year.

BJORN: Not me!

ABBA ★ 1977	
SINGLES	**REACHED**
Knowing Me, Knowing You	UK No. 1
Dancing Queen	US No. 1
Knowing Me, Knowing You	US No. 14
The Name of the Game	UK No. 1
ALBUMS	**REACHED**
Arrival	UK No. 1
Arrival	US No. 20

1978

THE BEE GEES

THE BEE GEES STORY *was a five-part series produced by Terry Warrick and recorded mainly in America by Paul Gambaccini in 1978 — the peak of the band's success.*

'The interviews with the Gibb brothers were done in Florida,' he recalls. 'Such was the success of the band at the time that I remember arriving at Barry's house, which faced on to the sea, to find people installing a radar security system to ensure that nobody sailed up and kidnapped any of his family.

'They themselves recognised that with Saturday Night Fever *they had been ludicrously successful, especially in America. But they were very objective about it and, because they had been at the bottom as well, they knew how to cope with it.*

'The series ended with a reference to the enormous advance orders for their Sgt Pepper *cover album. Little did we know that it would be a disaster. I think personally that the biggest problem for them was that* Saturday Night Fever *had branded them with a particular sound, and it took them a long time to re-establish themselves again.'*

GAMBACCINI [NARRATING]: The brothers Gibb — Barry, Maurice and Robin — started recording when they were teenagers and were international hit-makers before they were twenty-one. By the time they were in their late twenties they had been on top three times and washed up twice. When they became the bestselling recording act in the world in 1978, they had already been singing together for over two decades. Their first attempts to make it as a group were in Australia, but it wasn't until they came back to Britain that they found the winning formula.

BARRY: We sent our tapes to Brian, Brian Epstein. We sent all the stuff to Eppy straight away, 'cause that's who we thought was the governor. He was the tops in managers. We sent copies of the songs and everything, and Robert Stigwood picked them up in the office one day because he was the managing director of NEMS, where Brian was the chairman. He'd always wanted his Beatles, you know, his own group. Where Brian was always taken up with the boys, Robert wanted his own boys. So he picked it up and read the date when we were arriving. He listened to all the songs we'd written and the stuff we'd recorded, and he was more or less taken up with our songwriting more than anything. But when he saw our act, which we used to do in the clubs in Australia, which he understood by being Australian, he knew right away that there was something there that he liked, and on the Friday we signed a five-year contract with NEMS.

GAMBACCINI: **Their first UK-recorded LP, called *Bee Gees First*, gave Robert's 'boys' hits on both sides of the Atlantic, with 'New York Mining Disaster 1941' and 'To Love Somebody'.**

MAURICE: That [LP] was very Beatles influenced. In those days, just about everybody was copying the Beatles to a great extent and we were not any different. Everybody loved the Beatles and everyone was influenced by them.

GAMBACCINI: **While they were in America promoting their first album, the brothers began writing their next release, 'Massachusetts'. The song recorded, the brothers took it to Robert Stigwood and Brian Epstein. Maurice remembers the encounter.**

ALL IN THE FAMILY – (LEFT TO RIGHT) BARRY GIBB, MAURICE,
SISTER LESLEY, LITTLE BROTHER ANDY,
MUM BARBARA AND ROBIN

MAURICE: It was the last time I saw Brian, because on the Sunday he was found dead. He was supposed to join us in Cannes the next day. He came out of his office and said, 'That "Massachusetts" is going to be the world's Number One.' He said, 'It's beautiful.' And walked away. That's the last words he ever said to me.

GAMBACCINI: **Brian Epstein proved a seer. 'Massachusetts' reached the top of the British chart in October 1967 and the Bee Gees were finally in the first division of the world's pop stars.**

GAMBACCINI: **More hits followed with 'Words' and 'Holiday', but Robin Gibb wasn't completely pleased with the reputation songs like 'Words' gave the Bee Gees.**

ROBIN: When we started getting hits with ballads like 'Words' and things like that, we felt a little claustrophobic. We felt people were just fed up with listening to these sort of slushy ballads coming out. It was not what we wanted to do. But people would automatically say, 'Yes, release that, because it's a ballad and they identify with you and ballads.' And we got stuck in the end.

GAMBACCINI: **After a flop with the single 'Jumbo', the next song the Gibbs wrote became their second British Number One and their first American Top Ten hit, 'I Just Gotta Get a Message to You'. Barry admits it was morbid.**

BARRY: We like to assume identities, we still do today, we assume identities. The songs we write have nothing to do with ourselves. In that case it was a guy on Death Row. We thought, 'Well, what must he be thinking about? Whoever's on Death Row, what would he be thinking about? And how would you like to be in that situation, you know?' So we wrote a song like that. Not a lot of people can relate to it, but a lot of people on Death Row did!

GAMBACCINI: **By the time of their fifth album, *Odessa*, in 1969, the group had hit problems. The English-speaking world loved the album's velvet red cover, but not the music.**

MAURICE: It became a sort of concept album here. People thought it was an in-depth album like, 'What do you mean by those lyrics?' It wasn't misunderstood, it was just never finished. We never finished it. It was on the verge of the time we were splitting up, and we never got around to finishing it. It was a four-sided album and there was just us three doing it. We were already falling apart and fighting and all that situation. So it really never got polished off. I think it was a good album. It just seemed to drift on to nowhere, instead of coming to the right climax.

GAMBACCINI: **The Bee Gees had stumbled professionally. Personally they were falling victim to more severe strains. They began to fight with each other.**

103

★

ROBIN: We were very young and we didn't know how to handle it — that was all it was. It was like a kettle that just had to boil. I think it was good for us to split up when we did.

GAMBACCINI: **The Bee Gees had issued a flop album and a stiff single. Now their internal discontent exploded. They broke up, as much as brothers can ever break up. Robin went solo and the British music press had a field day.**

ROBIN: Groups can split up all the time now and come back together again, and no one bats an eyelid or says anything. They just made a hell of a hoo-ha out of it when we did. It was never a hoo-ha in America when we split up, but it was here. For some unknown reason, it was murder. It was the biggest nightmare that I've ever, ever gone through, and for the three of us. The press here, the trade papers and everyone, just made our lives hell. They made it so bad for us when we got back together again. I'll never forget those days. I could never understand why people wrote and said the things they did about us, when all we did was break up.

GAMBACCINI: **Because they were brothers, the Gibbs would inevitably be speaking to each other regularly. The press wanted to know what each had said. And then what each thought about what the others had said.**

ROBIN: It was such a dreadful situation at that time because nobody knew what was going to happen from day to day. I never even enjoyed the success of [solo album] *Saved by the Bell*, even in this country, because I was too busy in my lawyer's office. Everybody was suing each other — it was ridiculous. The only people that were benefiting were the lawyers.

MAURICE: We couldn't appear on a TV show without anyone saying, 'Where's your brothers?', 'When are you guys coming back together again?' Nobody in the business wanted us to be apart. I don't know if that's love or hate [LAUGHS], but we were talked into coming back together again. We weren't ready to come back together again when we did. It took us five years to get our heads back to where we were long before we broke up, before all that ego business started.

GAMBACCINI: **The pressures of being apart had proved worse than the pressures of being together. And there was no question that the quality of the music had suffered. In 1970 the brothers decided to give each other one more chance.**

BARRY: There was never any question that the Bee Gees wouldn't come back together again. There was never a question of that. But there's no question in my mind that the three of us could have made it independently, separately, given enough time. At the time we all went solo, within fifteen months we were back together again. Give each of us two or three years, we might have all made it independently anyway. But the public did not want to know about the Bee Gees being independent, separate artists. They only wanted to know about the Bee Gees together. That was one thing that made it real hard for us. The other thing was the press would not forget the Bee Gees. They wouldn't let us be Barry Gibb, Maurice Gibb or Robin Gibb. To this day, Maurice believes that none of us could make it better without each other. I believe that every one of us could make it. The same as [younger brother] Andy's doing now. But the Bee Gees are better off together. The combination of the three of our talents put together is a lot stronger.

GAMBACCINI: **'How Can You Mend a Broken Heart?' was an American Number One in the summer of 1971. It was the Bee Gees' biggest US hit to date and, after 'Lonely Days', their second consecutive American smash. But in Britain it meant nothing, and the brothers began to think they might have to leave England.**

BARRY: 'Broken Heart' was just after we came back together and I still think they didn't want to know. That's really all I can chalk it up to. We've always cared about the British fans, but we just had to get away because they wouldn't accept us. Even our fans weren't accepting us. We had to get away, we had to get to a place where people didn't know all these stories of our arguments and all this business.

GAMBACCINI: **Barry knew it and Maurice knew it too. Their greatest hit had flopped at home, where people thought of the Bee Gees in the past tense.**

MAURICE: I'm sure half of them [DJs] thought that we really weren't going to stay together too long so, 'I don't think it's worth playing them'. Because I think half of them still thought we were broken up.

GAMBACCINI: **The Bee Gees continued to work on ballads. In retrospect Barry could see the group was getting stuck in a rut.**

BARRY: We were on speed and all that business — we didn't know. We'd just simply gone off the road. We didn't know what was selling, we didn't listen to other people's records. We didn't know what was current, we were writing what we thought the Bee Gees fans would go for. We didn't think that there were other people who were not Bee Gees fans that maybe would be if we'd just done something different.

GAMBACCINI: **'My World' and 'Run to Me' were moderate hits in the summer of 1972. After that, the Bee Gees slumped.**

ROBIN: We started recording in the States at the end of '72. But I call these days the quiet days for the Bee Gees on both sides of the Atlantic because it was our transition period. We didn't expect immense success because we were getting out of the old Bee Gees. We wanted the old Bee Gees to go away. We wanted people just to forget about the old Bee Gees — that's the only way we could not suffocate. We just went completely underground and just concentrated on the roots of our music. And we had a couple of transitional albums which we weren't really happy with in this sort of '72–'74 period.

GAMBACCINI: **Recording had turned sour for the Bee Gees. Concerts did too. And that was the last straw.**

ROBIN: In 1974, things weren't really going very well for us at all. Not in America, and not here. We were playing Batley's Variety Club. It was a different Bee Gees altogether than it is now. And we thought, 'We've come to this, this is not us', and we just walked out. Because the people around us didn't know what we had to offer. So we walked out of that club and we never looked back. We said, 'That is never, ever going to happen to this group.' We know we've got so much to offer. We're creative people and that is not where it ends. We knew that. We walked out and we just packed up and left the country.

GAMBACCINI: **So with new musical resolve, what direction were 'the new Bee Gees' to take?**

MAURICE: Our root was R&B music, not disco, but R&B music, but we didn't know what direction it was that we were more positive in. We loved country & western music and things like that. So we made up an album in *Main Course*, which was several directions — country, with songs like 'Come on Over', and R&B with songs like 'Nights on Broadway' and 'Jive Talkin'.' The most positive thing that came off that album was the R&B, and that really just paved the whole way. That's what we wanted to do and we just thanked God that that's what people accepted.

GAMBACCINI: **'Jive Talkin'' was the Bee Gees' second American Number One. But this one was also a Top Five hit in Britain.**

MAURICE: Nobody knew it was us at all and eventually when it came to light that it was us, once again the British radio woke up to the fact that, 'Good grief, this is a good one from the Bee Gees, isn't it?' They all suddenly went, 'Ah, that's a little different', and we realised that that field was also successful for us. Even though all that time we could play music like that, we were always scared to release that sort of R&B-cum-danceable music because we thought the public didn't want it from us. Disco music wasn't very big when 'Jive Talkin'' came out. Then *Billboard* adopted a disco chart, and I think *Record World* did too. And 'You Should Be Dancing' was a very big disco record. It was Number One in the disco charts for eighteen weeks.

THE BROTHERS GIBB – 'SUCCESS SO GREAT IT SET NEW STANDARDS'

GAMBACCINI: 'You Should Be Dancing' laid the groundwork for a future direction for the Bee Gees. It became a disco anthem – and that's what it was meant to be.

ROBIN: We thought, 'Let's just do a record to dance to.' 'Jive Talkin'' was never a disco record, although it's being used in the film as a disco record, but it was never a disco record. It was never a disco hit. But with 'You Should Be Dancing', we said, 'Let's make a dance record.'

GAMBACCINI: Nik Cohn, an English writer based in New York, had told Robert Stigwood he'd send him ideas for movies. Stigwood saw Cohn's *New York* magazine cover story about disco-mania in New York City, called him back and said, 'Who needs ideas, let's do your magazine piece.' He then rang the brothers at the Honky Château in France.

BARRY: He rang us up and he said, 'Would you like to do the soundtrack to a film? It's a film I'm making, I haven't got a title. Can you also think of that?' [LAUGHS] So I said, 'How many songs?' He said, 'Oh, about six or seven.' 'Well,' I said, 'that's one a day. What about a script for the film?' He said, 'The script hasn't even been completed yet.' I said, 'Look, we'll just get on with the soundtrack.' So we put the phone down and we went to work. We wrote these songs in French at the château, right out in the middle of the country. Howling winds, it was awful, it was like a Spanish jail. To this day I don't even know why we were there, but we were there and we wrote. It was very productive.

GAMBACCINI: Perhaps the most productive week in showbusiness history.

ROBIN: 'Stayin' Alive' was about survival in a big city, any big city, but basically New York. It worked so well with the film that when we saw the film even we were surprised. It just amazed us that we'd never seen the script ourselves and there it was.

GAMBACCINI: 'Stayin' Alive' was Number One in the United States for four weeks, sold over two million copies and started climbing singles charts in countries all over the world, whether the locals spoke English or not. With the success of this single, it became apparent that this group of songs was making the Bee Gees more successful than they had ever been before. In one week, the three American charts had three different Number Ones – Samantha Sang's 'Emotion', written by the Bee Gees; brother Andy's '(Love is) Thicker than Water', co-written by Barry; and the Bee Gees' own single. It was the only time the three most important charts had three different Number Ones, all produced by the same people. But the following week, that Bee Gees 45 was Number One on all three charts and stayed there for nearly two months. It was the song that helped answer the question, 'What are we going to call this movie?'

BARRY: Robert wanted to call the film 'Saturday Night' and we had the song 'Night Fever'. So we told him we didn't like 'Saturday Night' and Robert didn't want to just call it 'Night Fever' — he wanted to relate something to do with Saturday night. So he chewed it over and rang back and said, 'I'll compromise — Saturday Night Fever.' And we said, 'All right, that's great, so we'll keep it at that.'

CATCH THE FEVER ON FILM – 'ROBERT WANTED

TO CALL THE FILM SATURDAY NIGHT AND WE HAD A SONG CALLED "NIGHT FEVER"'

GAMBACCINI: 'Night Fever' was the Bee Gees' first British Number One in ten years. It helped make the Saturday Night Fever double album the bestselling LP ever. By the summer of '78 it had sold over sixteen million copies and the Bee Gees were the biggest money-makers in the history of the record business. 'If I Can't Have You', by Yvonne Elliman, completed one of the most incredible sequences in American chart history. Four tracks from the same album had become Number One singles. It was a first. But only one of many firsts achieved by Saturday Night Fever. The run of hit singles and the international success of the film promoted sales of the album long past the cut-off point of previous hit LPs, and by August Saturday Night Fever had sold twenty-two million copies, more than any album ever — and was still selling. It was an astonishing turnaround for a group that couldn't even sell one per cent of that four years before. Not every showbusiness cloud has a silver lining but, as Barry pointed out, their previously erratic fortunes had prepared the Bee Gees to handle their historic success.

BARRY: The whole going up, going down and going up business has been a total education for us because the people who we knew when we were originally what you might call at the top, when we went to the bottom, they all disappeared. And when we came up again, only the people that were with us when we were at the bottom stayed with us and those people that are with us today — our original road manager from ten years ago, Tom Kennedy, is still with us today; our personal manager, Dick Ashby, who started out as our road manager, is still with us today. And they went through all the ups and downs too. And when the Bee Gees were lucky to get a gig in Batley's, those guys were still there.

It's good that the glamour goes away. Then you know when you get the glamour, it's a façade. There's no such thing as real glamour, it's just the way other people look at you. We learned the business and the business has to be a part of it all, the business has to be the common denominator, it has to be the strongest thing. Everything is based on money. All of showbusiness is based on how rich you can get and how fast. That's just something we never knew. In those early years it's something we definitely never knew. You know, we made money, we spent a lot of money. But we didn't know how we'd gotten it and how fast and how much other people were making off our backs.

GAMBACCINI: It was a long way from the dog days of 1970 to the money-making months of 1978. A success so great it simply set new standards for the music business.

THE BEE GEES ★ 1978

SINGLES	REACHED
How Deep Is Your Love	US No. 1
How Deep Is Your Love	UK No. 3
Stayin' Alive	US No. 1
Stayin' Alive	UK No. 4
Night Fever	US No. 1
Night Fever	UK No. 1
Oh Darlin' (Robin only)	US No. 15
Too Much Heaven	UK No. 3

ALBUMS	REACHED
Saturday Night Fever	US No. 1
Saturday Night Fever	UK No. 1
Sgt Pepper's Lonely Hearts Club Band	UK No. 38
Sgt Pepper's Lonely Hearts Club Band	US No. 5

1980

JOHN LENNON

THE LENNON TAPES, *produced by Doreen Davies and Paul Williams, in five parts, was planned in 1980 as a landmark series for Radio 1. John Lennon had been away from the music scene for five years. Now, he was relaunching his career with the album Double Fantasy. Little did DJ Andy Peebles know as he flew out to New York to talk to the Lennons that on the return flight he would receive the news that John had been shot dead only hours after the interview. The tapes in the bag on Andy's lap became more than a landmark. They were to provide the only commentary in Lennon's own words on the final five years of his life.*

'John didn't enjoy the prospect of being interviewed,' remembers Andy, 'but I think he eventually agreed because the BBC had meant so much to him since the early days of the Beatles. Even so, we didn't get final permission to do the interview until we'd had a meeting with Yoko two days beforehand. She was charming but tough, and like John was fully aware that they needed to do the interview to promote the new album, Double Fantasy.

'John had been away from the scene for five years, and was nervous about being judged all over again. He knew in his own mind that he couldn't afford to come back and fail. I remember there had already been some criticism of the album, saying John was "toning down" his act, "softening up". I thought that was unfair — although it was a very different John we heard on Double Fantasy, there are some superb tracks on it. In the five years away, John seemed to have reappraised his life — he'd got his relationship with Yoko and with his two sons sorted out, and now he'd found a reason to be creative again. He went through all sorts of emotions in front of me during the interview, but generally I found him positive and enthusiastic about everything.'

PEEBLES: **Five years is an awful long time. What sort of mental discipline did it involve resisting picking up a guitar?**

DJ ANDY PEEBLES MEETS JOHN AND YOKO IN THE STUDIO BEFORE RECORDING LENNON'S LAST INTERVIEW

LENNON: Well, it wasn't a matter of resisting. The first half-year or year, I had this sort of feeling in the back of my mind that I ought to, and I'd go through periods of panic, because I was not in the *NME* [*New Musical Express*] or *Billboard*, or being seen at Studio 54 with Mick and Bianca. I just didn't exist any more. I got a little fear of that. It would come like a paranoia, then it would go away because I'd be involved with the baby or involved with whatever other business we were involved with. But that only lasted about nine months, and then suddenly it went away, and I realised there was a life after death.

PEEBLES: **Did you enjoy that realisation?**

LENNON: It was great. I would sit around thinking, 'What does this remind me of? This reminds me of being fifteen.' I didn't have to write songs at fifteen. I wrote if I wanted to, played rock 'n' roll if I wanted to. I didn't *have* to do it. I didn't have some imaginary standard set up by me or by some group of critics, or whatever.

PEEBLES: **In other words, back to the days before the pressure started?**

LENNON: Yes. So it was before. I sort of got back to that and that's when I suddenly could do it again with ease. The most enjoyable thing for me is the inspiration, because the songs really come when you're not sitting down like a craftsman writing. I can do that, you know. You want a song about bananas for a movie? I could do that OK. I'm quite capable of turning it out like that. I wouldn't enjoy it so much, maybe, but I could do it on that level. But my joy is when you're possessed, like a medium. I'll be sitting round and it'll come in the middle of the night or at a time when you don't want it to. That's the exciting part. So I'm lying around and then this thing comes as a whole piece, you know: words and music. And I think, 'Well, can I say I wrote it?' I don't know who the hell wrote it. I'm just sitting here and this whole damned song comes out. So it's like you're driven and

★

you find yourself over a piano or guitar and you put it down because it's been given to you.

PEEBLES: **Yoko, how did you find him during this period? Were you relieved that he'd finally decided to lay down his guitar and rest?**

ONO: Well, we weren't suffering or we weren't feeling worried when we were just relaxing, so there was no strong feeling of relief. In fact, the nicest thing about *Double Fantasy* was that while we were making it we were fully aware that we didn't have to make it. We were making it and enjoying it, but we could always go back to the other life, because the thing was that we know that we have the other life as well. It's not like we always have to be in the front.

PEEBLES: **Were your friends very surprised when you adopted that stance as far as taking the five years off was concerned? I mean, was there any external pressure that people put on you and said, 'Come on, John, what's happening?'**

LENNON: There was a lot. You remember when you asked me, I think it was off-mike before we started, 'Have you got any English friends in town?' Well, suddenly when Mick Jagger or David Bowie or Elton John came to town, I wouldn't respond, because they'd always want me to go down to the studio or to the clubs, and I didn't want to get in there again. Or Harry Nilsson, you know. It's like birds of a feather. So I didn't want to go back to that pressure part of my life again.

PEEBLES: **You said that you reversed roles, that John looked after Sean. How good a cook are you, John?**

LENNON: Not bad. Not great. I've mastered the art of rice. They say anyone can cook rice, but few people can cook it well. I can cook it reasonably well. I can do fish.

ONO: You're a good bread-maker.

LENNON: I've learned to make bread, which I was thrilled with. I took a Polaroid of my first bread. I couldn't believe they came out like that.

ONO: In a good old macho tradition, he had to record it for history.

LENNON: I was thrilled, it's not macho. Anybody would. It was the first bread. It looked great, and it tasted good. That was pretty damned good, and so for about half a year or a year I was providing food for Yoko, the baby, even the staff was eating. I was so excited that I could do it that I would bring all the staff in to eat lunch. But after a bit it was wearing me out, because life becomes, as all housewives know . . .

LENNON AT WORK ON *DOUBLE FANTASY* – 'HE KNEW HE COULDN'T AFFORD
TO COME BACK AND FAIL'

ONO: . . . a routine.

LENNON: . . . a routine between the meals, you see. You think from breakfast
. . . once the baby's had the breakfast, you've got a little time to yourself for coffee
and a smoke or whatever, then everybody comes up and wants to eat. OK, feed
them. You don't get a gold record. They just swallow it. If they swallow it, that means
you were a hit. If they don't swallow it, that means you did something wrong. It
was a Zen experience to master that cooking thing and put as much energy into
that bread and make it right.

So this went on for about nine months. I really enjoyed it, because I concentrated.
I put my mind to it. But it's the meals, the meals is what you live, you live a regulation
between meals. And on the other side of me, there was always just being served
by women – whether it was my Auntie Mimi (God bless you, wherever you are),
or whoever – served by females, wives, girlfriends. It was quite an experience, and
I appreciated what women have done for me all my life. I'd never even thought
about it. But I enjoyed it. I looked on it as a discipline, an absolute discipline, and
that's how I approached it. Through that I got into a whole other new world.

PEEBLES: **And one of the most important facets of that world surely was that
it gave you a great deal of time to spend with your son, Sean.**

LENNON: Yes, because between Yoko and I . . . I can't do figures and numbers.
I'm not good at business, and somebody had to take care of business, whether it

was Beatles, Apples or surviving inflation or whatever you call it. And there's no way I can do it. I don't have the talent. So she had to do it. She has the talent to do it. And so I had to contribute something, not just sit around either talking about the former greatness of the Beatles, or the fact that I'm not writing songs, so what am I supposed to do? So I had the sort of sibling . . . the early relationship with Sean. Because she would go to the office, even though the office was only downstairs in the same building, she was still not there. So Sean and I would spend this time together. And it was fantastic.

PEEBLES: **Well, as I sit here talking to you, you look two very happy people. Which of you, or was it both of you, who first got in touch with David Geffen?**

LENNON: He [Geffen] made the contacts. She did the deal.

ONO: We decided to meet and so he came to my office, and sort of . . . I was checking him, you know, he was all right.

LENNON: You see, the point about me cooking and her doing the business, before we'd always had somebody come in to look after the business, and you know the story of that. It's all . . .

PEEBLES: **. . . history.**

LENNON: Some lawyer or some accountant would come in and say, 'I'll handle it all for you.' Since 1962 they've been handling it, and then nothing but tax problems and whatever. There's a long history of it. Like we don't own any of the Beatles' songs, we don't own any of the Beatles' records, we've got farthings for royalties, and all the rest of it. Anyway, the point being we decided not to have an outside party. We had to look after our own stuff and face that reality. She could deal with it, so I could go to the other side, which I could deal with. I'm a homeboy, I always like to hang around the house.

PEEBLES: **So along came Mr Geffen, and you made the decision to record the album** *Double Fantasy*, **which we've been hearing a lot recently.**

LENNON: We decided to make it first, then answer all the letters and enquiries that came, wanting to have the album. We eliminated the ones that said, 'Can we hear it first?' OK, you can go to hell, forget about him, you know. If you can't trust us after all those years, forget it. I don't want to know about it. Also he [Geffen] wasn't a big company, so you weren't dealing with this anonymous grey suit.

PEEBLES: **In this stage of negotiation, did the old fear come back from the old days, that you were having to take a step that involved somebody else?**

LENNON: It did, yes. I was terrified. I was saying, 'Can we put it out without . . . without putting it out? Couldn't we do something else? Do I have to put my name on the paper?' Because I've only, you know, for the last five years . . . the first time I didn't owe somebody songs or records for the last fifteen or twenty years. Since 1962 I was signed up to somebody or other, and thankful to be, in 1962. But when you sign when you are twenty-one and it goes on for twenty years, and they all own you, life and soul, and you can never get out of it. . . . So I liked the five years when I was free of any contractual obligation. When she finally says, 'Look, you are going to have to sign something to say that they have the right to put the record out', I was saying, 'You're sure? Why don't you sign it? You put your name on it, I don't want to put my name on it.' But we made arrangements which didn't make me feel paranoid, because I don't want to owe people anything. The point of being a musician or artist to me was the freedom.

PEEBLES: **Do you feel now at this stage, here we are in December 1980, that the ease of writing is now back with you?**

LENNON: Yes.

PEEBLES: **And that you're going to be extremely prolific in the months and years to come?**

LENNON: Yes, I think it's going to be the one period when they say, 'Those two will do anything for publicity. For Christ's sake, get them off the front pages.' People were bitching at us because we were always doing something, and then they were bitching at us because we weren't doing anything. And I have a funny feeling that it's going to be the other way round again, because we're talking and talking and talking, and we have all sorts of plans and ideas in our heads. It's just a matter of getting it done. And I'm sorry about you people that get fed up of hearing about us, but, you know, we like to do it, so it's too bad.

JOHN LENNON ★ 1980

SINGLES	REACHED
(Just Like) Starting Over	UK No. 1
(Just Like) Starting Over	US No. 1
Happy Christmas (War Is Over)	UK No. 4
(later No. 2 in Jan 1981)	
Imagine	UK No. 9
(later No. 1 in Jan 1981)	

ALBUMS	REACHED
Double Fantasy	UK No. 1
Double Fantasy	US No. 1

JOHN AND YOKO IN 1980 – 'WE HAVE ALL SORTS OF PLANS AND IDEAS IN OUR HEADS.

IT'S JUST A MATTER OF GETTING IT DONE'

1983

THE POLICE

DAVID 'KID' JENSEN, host of Radio 1's mid-evening show in the early eighties, helped to break a large number of bands, including the Police. By 1983, they had already had their greatest hits and were beginning to move off into various solo projects. However, on the night of 16 May 1983, they were together in the Radio 1 studios talking to Jensen about their new album, Synchronicity, with Mike Hawkes producing.

'I'd gained something of a reputation as a supporter of the Police since their early days,' Jensen remembers. 'I guess it was that distinctive fusion of reggae and rock which appealed to me. They were really one of the few groups to emerge from punk origins (a) who survived, and (b) who actually had something to say in interviews. They had had absolutely enormous success all around the world, and by 1983 I think they were feeling that they had done everything a rock group could do. They all had their various solo work, like Sting and his acting, which had caused a great deal of speculation as to whether the Police were splitting up. Despite the uncertainty about the future, I found them all good interviewees, as articulate and intelligent as you could wish rock stars to be.'

JENSEN: Stuart, Andy and Sting, welcome back to Radio 1. There were reports as recently as a month or two ago that the band was going to split up, because you all seemed to be involved in solo projects. But you did take a bit of time off from each other, didn't you?

SUMMERS: I think that's necessary, like a marriage, where the only way to keep the marriage together is to take a little time off. Doing solo projects really adds to the longevity. We're into our sixth year this summer, so if you imagine the amount of hours we've actually spent in cars and hotel rooms together, it's phenomenal. So at this point I think it's only healthy that we spend time apart, but it certainly doesn't mean that we're splitting up.

JENSEN: So let's go way back. Stuart, you were the founder member of the Police.

COPELAND: Guilty, as charged.

JENSEN: That was in 1977?

COPELAND: That's right, at the end of 1976, beginning of 1977.

JENSEN: It was a fairly punky scene in those days. Was it your intention to play punk music?

COPELAND: No, we didn't want to play punk music. We just wanted to play the punk clubs, because they were the only kind of places that you could play, unless you had a record company and could play the colleges.

JENSEN: Do you remember your first gig?

STING: Our first gig was in Cardiff. We played thirty songs in fifteen minutes. It was hilarious.

JENSEN: Whose songs were you playing, because you hadn't known each other that long, so you weren't collaborating, were you?

COPELAND: We started off with my songs. We had to convince Sting that he was joining a group. It was supposed to already be a group. We had to have material, so I said, 'OK, here's the material', which was all just one or two chords. That was the set, that was the material.

JENSEN: How soon after that did 'Fall Out' come out, because that's the indie single that a lot of fans are not even aware of?

COPELAND: That was step two. Having conned the musicians into joining a group, then we had to make a record, so I borrowed some money from a friend, and we went into Pathway Studios and recorded it.

119

★

JENSEN: **Really soon after that, you established your style. You picked up on reggae rhythms. Who in particular in the field of reggae do you guys admire?**

STING: Bob Marley was the man who introduced reggae to almost everybody. He was a great crossover artist. It's a great loss that he's actually not with us any more.

SUMMERS: I think Jimmy Cliff made a big impression on me, as well as Bob Marley.

JENSEN: **Are you acknowledged at all in Jamaica?**

STING: I heard our records a lot when I was in Jamaica. All over the Caribbean they play our records.

SUMMERS: Certainly when you go out to record in Montserrat, as we've done twice, you get the feeling that the Police are more acceptable there than some other kinds of rock music, because of that kind of crossover thing.

JENSEN: **You were the first band to really succeed in this field. Other bands tried using reggae in other ways, and didn't have the success you had.**

SUMMERS: The difference between us playing it and a lot of other groups — this is not a trumpet-blowing thing — but to us it was a means of getting somewhere else. Not to copy reggae, and make it a huge part of our style. It was a way of approaching the use of guitar, bass and drums, and trying to change the traditional trio sound — away from the heavy sort of sheet sound of someone like Hendrix or Eric Clapton or Cream. We wanted a different sound out of the trio. The reggae enabled us to get into that approach. What makes the Police is that there are so many disparate influences and different strands. . . .

COPELAND: Desperate influences, too.

SUMMERS: It comes out of the difference and the diversity of the backgrounds. Not the similarities.

STING: It might have made records easier to make, in fact, if we'd all been of the same mind, but the fact that we're not — which is the cause of a lot of argument — is also the cause of the dynamic in the group which has made us very successful.

JENSEN: **Your first hit was 'Roxanne', but that had to be reissued to become a hit. On whose instigation was it reissued?**

STING: That's an accident of history, because it was a hit in America first, or a relative hit, and we came back to England with that 'glory' under our belts, saying, 'We've had a hit in America.' So they thought they'd re-release it in England to see what happens. And sure enough, it paid off.

JENSEN: Another record at about that time was reissued to become a hit. That was 'Can't Stand Losing You'. Was that the same story, a hit abroad and then . . . ?

STING: I think that was *your* instigation, actually. It was Kid Jensen's Record of the Week.

COPELAND: I remember jumping up and down somewhere in a studio, going, 'Wow, Kid Jensen likes us.'

SUMMERS: You had the taste and urbanity back then to recognise it.

STING: We salute you, Kid — or David, or whatever you're called nowadays.

. . . .

THE POLICE – STING, COPELAND AND SUMMERS – 'TRYING TO CHANGE
THE TRADITIONAL TRIO SOUND'

JENSEN: You can call me Mr Jensen. 1979 was a good year, because in autumn you had your first Number One single, which was 'Message in a Bottle', from the LP *Regatta de Blanc*, which allegedly you went into the studio without rehearsing and without having any songs written.

COPELAND: That's the way we do all our albums. The songs are written, but we don't rehearse or arrange them until we get into the studio.

JENSEN: Isn't that very expensive?

COPELAND: No, we were known for how cheaply we recorded.

SUMMERS: When we recorded that album, we'd gone through our first major flush of success, and we'd been on the road for something like nine months, so going into the studio for the second album was a whole different story from the first one. We were much better. We were really into playing. We'd been playing for months and months in America. We were hot.

JENSEN: The LP brought you a couple of Number Ones – 'Walking on the Moon' was also Number One in the UK. Are both those numbers still ones that you enjoy playing live?

SUMMERS: That's still my favourite number to actually play. It gives me the biggest thrill, the biggest spine-tingle.

JENSEN: Because you do have to improvise a lot, don't you? I suppose that keeps it fairly interesting – unlike some artists who play note for note exactly as it appeared on record.

SUMMERS: It's a combination of really wanting to take the risks on stage, and also having a slightly sloppy attitude to discipline. We tend to go on, and things occur. We always leave that spontaneous moment to arise, which it does . . . once or twice a year.

JENSEN: Sting, in recent months you have been the most visible member of the Police, because we've been reading about all sorts of things, about your personal life. I get the impression that it's an aspect of success that you're not overly fond of.

STING: Frankly, I've stopped reading the papers that produce this kind of thing, so I'm not affected by it. I don't know what they print. They invent a private life for you, and then they comment on it. They can do what they like. It's not me they're talking about, it's some invention.

JENSEN: But what about the way your audiences will then perceive you? Is that not important, even if you don't believe it?

STING: I think the audiences listen to the music. Whether or not the papers print me as a bad boy, I've still got a good voice and I write good songs. That's all that matters.

JENSEN: **Something that you have been working on recently is *Dune*, which is a science fiction picture, which I know nothing about.**

STING: I'm playing a bad guy.

JENSEN: **You were a bad guy in *Brimstone and Treacle* as well.**

STING: I'm just a bad guy all the time. I don't have to act. *Dune* is probably one of the most famous science fiction books written in the past twenty years, by a man called Frank Herbert. The film, because it's such a large project, is costing fifty million dollars, which is something of a record. They're making it in Mexico, so the dollar can go further. Even if it's a lousy film, it'll be an event. That amount of money cannot go unnoticed.

COPELAND: Sting's getting most out of it.

JENSEN: **When you guys are away in America, doing films or playing with other people, or just on holiday, do you make it a point at all to keep up with the music trends in the UK?**

STING IN *DUNE* – 'EVEN IF IT'S A LOUSY FILM, IT'LL BE AN EVENT'

COPELAND: It's really hard to. They move so fast. Every time we come back from a tour, we feel provincial. You look at *Top of the Pops*, and ten out of twenty groups in the Top Twenty you've never heard of before. England has better access for new bands to the charts than anywhere else in the world, and that's what makes England such a vibrant place musically. That's why all the big trends come out of England.

JENSEN: I think you're right. Having been away from this country for a long time, because things change so fast, did you ever have any doubts about whether people would still love you?

SUMMERS: Obviously, when we go away we don't want to get in an ivory tower, or be so smug that when we come back we don't think we've got to work really hard, or really try to keep the edge in our music. But at the same time, you can go crazy if you try and listen to every new band that comes out, or to try to stay with the pop charts all the time, because it proliferates so much in England. It's truly impossible. Really we have to think about our own music more than anything else, and try to keep that alive. I don't think it comes from listening to the latest pop group that comes out every week in England. You find a few major ones that you really think are interesting. You find your peers and you see what's happening. I've only found so far three or four things that have truly turned me on. I watched Aztec Camera the other night on BBC2. I thought they were great, I really enjoyed them. I like the Creatures' new single, and Big Country.

JENSEN: What about playing live for you, because you've played live since 1977, and you've worked very hard? Not just America and Europe, but you made history when you went to some of the Far Eastern countries. Are you now itching to get going again?

SUMMERS: Yes, I'm really looking forward to it. We rehearsed in Los Angeles a few weeks back, and that was fun. We'll be starting in July.

STING: We're doing some dates in England, but we hope to do a major English tour round about Christmas. Playing stuff from the new album.

JENSEN: Listen, the LP – why the title Synchronicity? You mentioned that these things even years ago were happening to your life.

STING: Some of the best things that happen in music happen by accident. Particularly with three musicians. When you improvise, sometimes by accident you get some amazing things that you couldn't organise. 'Synchronicity' is a theory about coincidence. We feel that that was related to the music somehow. There are lots of coincidences in our careers. It makes you think about destiny. Maybe we were destined to become a big group.

SYNCHRONICITY, NUMBER ONE IN THE UK AND US, BUT 'AT THIS POINT, IT'S ONLY HEALTHY THAT WE SPEND TIME APART'

JENSEN: Are you guys intending to stay together as a unit after this tour?

STING: After this interview, probably not.

COPELAND: Let's not get confused about this thing about our solo projects. The solo projects are what keep us together. If it weren't for the solo projects, we would go crazy.

SUMMERS: I don't think of them as solo projects. We're three guys, we're in a band, and we also have lives. We do other things as well. Starting in July, we'll be touring for six or seven months. That's a lot of work together. Then naturally, we're going to need a break for a while. But it's nice for us to go off and do other things, because sometimes it's just as refreshing to work on another project as to go on holiday.

STING: I think we've all maintained our freedom as individuals and as a group to say, 'Well, if tomorrow we don't feel like being a group, we won't be.' It's not as if we have to be a group to breathe the air. We're not joined at the hip. We have lives that are separate.

THE POLICE ★ 1983

SINGLES	REACHED
Every Breath You Take	UK No. 1
Every Breath You Take	US No. 1
Wrapped Around Your Finger	UK No. 7
Wrapped Around Your Finger	US No. 8
Synchronicity II	UK No. 17
King of Pain	US No. 3
Synchronicity II	US No. 16

ALBUMS	REACHED
Synchronicity	UK No. 1
Synchronicity	US No. 1

1984-86

BOB GELDOF

RICHARD SKINNER'S evening show on Radio 1 had a long-standing appointment with Bob Geldof for 24 November 1984 to talk about his new album. Quite by chance, it was the night before the recording of a track Bob had planned with Midge Ure of Ultravox called 'Do They Know It's Christmas?', which they had asked friends in the business to help them with in order to raise money for the famine in Ethiopia. The next day, Bob & Co. set in motion a series of events which changed the face of pop music, smashing records and saving thousands of lives along the way. 'Do They Know It's Christmas?' became Britain's bestselling single ever. It spawned an American version, a global live concert, and a style of fund-raising which has provided inspiration for countless other events.

Here, Bob's own words are selected from various Radio 1 interviews at key stages over the Band Aid/Live Aid period. Little did Richard Skinner know as he talked to Bob about the planned single that seven months later his would be the voice heard by an estimated six billion people around the world as he opened the global broadcast of Live Aid from Wembley Stadium.

'When I heard the line-up Bob was hoping to get for the single, I had my doubts whether it would ever happen at all,' he recalls. 'There had been nothing like it before. Later, on the day before Live Aid, I remember standing with Bob on the stage at Wembley at the moment when it dawned on him how much money would actually be raised on the day. He turned to me and said, "Do you realise how much cash you could make if you were doing this for yourself?" But of course, no one was doing it for themselves, that's what made it so special. All the artists set aside their showbiz personas and just got on with it.'

BOB AND THE STARS OF BAND AID. 'I PHONED EVERYBODY I
KNEW AND TO MY SURPRISE THEY ALL WANTED TO DO IT.'

SKINNER: **Bob Geldof is here, and Bob is talking not as a member of the Boomtown Rats, but as the instigator of a fascinating idea to raise money for the Ethiopian famine appeal. Perhaps you'd like to describe what you're up to.**

GELDOF: What we're up to is getting as many people from British pop music as possible to sing on a song that Midge Ure from Ultravox and myself have written called 'Do They Know It's Christmas?' I went around and phoned up everybody I knew, and much to my surprise they all wanted to do it, so tomorrow when we actually start recording, we'll have Spandau Ballet, Duran Duran, Wham!, Sting, the Style Council, Ultravox, the Young Ones, Heaven 17, Bananarama, Status Quo, maybe – fingers crossed – David Bowie, maybe Culture Club will be in on time, the Rats. . . . Who else?

SKINNER: **There are fourteen different acts so far.**

GELDOF: Oh, U2, sorry. They're flying in tomorrow for it. And on the B side, we've got McCartney, Frankie Goes to Hollywood, Jagger . . . I don't know.

SKINNER: **It sounds like a nightmare pulling it together, Bob.**

GELDOF: It was, but great fun. I just thought of it ten days ago. I have a low boredom threshold, so if it had gone on any longer I would have started getting bored. If I have a bee in my bonnet about something, I get cracking usually. But with Midge helping, it's been really good.

127

SKINNER: **Why not do a concert, as opposed to doing a record like this, because concerts can raise a lot of cash as well, and they're simpler in a lot of ways?**

GELDOF: Not really. If a band is going to play on stage, there's the technical things about using their own gear, so the changing between bands takes up to half an hour. Also, very few bands are going to play without their own gear, because they want to sound the best they can. For a concert, you have to hire the hall. No one's going to give it to you free. You have to hire the security. Also, with the record, everybody we've rung — not just the musicians — have immediately given us things for free. Like Trevor Horn and Joe Sinclair gave us SARM West [recording studio]. The people who print the labels on the sleeve are working for free. The guys from the factory at Phonogram have given up their weekends to work overtime for free. Peter Blake, the pop artist, who did the *Sgt Pepper* sleeve, is doing the sleeve for 'Do They Know It's Christmas?' Literally everybody. The TV crews who are doing the whole thing for us, they gave up their time. The T-shirt I'm wearing, which is the official 'Feed the World/Let Them Know It's Christmas' T-shirt, they are being printed up for free, and all the money we get from them goes into the fund. Robert Maxwell of the *Daily Mirror* is printing colour posters up. All the people playing — who are called Band Aid, by the way. . . .

SKINNER: [LAUGHS] **Fantastic.**

GELDOF: It started off where I thought that we'd make seventy grand, because that's how much you make roughly if you sell half a million records. It now looks like the record, because it's starting to sound very good, should do well. If we sell a million, along with all the other stuff, we might end up with a million and a half pounds.

SKINNER: **Wow. What happened with the Bangladesh concerts in the late seventies, of course, was a great lesson, because very little money in the end got through.**

GELDOF: Exactly. I spoke to George Harrison once, and I was asking about that, and he said it just got thrown away on legalities, and lawsuits, and then a very corrupt government in Dhaka, so the money never got through. What we've done is we've set up an independent trust fund, where if you buy this record, you can be guaranteed that the pound that you're giving will actually end up in somebody's mouth in Ethiopia.

SKINNER: **Are you overwhelmed by the response, because it sounds like it's absolutely incredible from every quarter?**

GELDOF: Yeah, it's gone from an idea in my head, wanting to do something other than put my hand in my pocket, to almost becoming an entire music industry thing. All the music press have said, 'Yes, free space.' The record retailers, I find it quite amazing that they've agreed to waive their profits.

SKINNER: **A very rare event.**

GELDOF: I don't think it's happened before. From every quarter, they just said, 'Yes, we'll help as much as we can.' And I think a lot of it has to do with the fact that it actually has nothing to do with what the song ends up like, there's almost a moral imperative to play it and indeed buy it. It doesn't become a question of taste.

SKINNER: **What sort of song is it?**

GELDOF: It's a Christmas song, in a standard vein. The words are, 'It's Christmas time, you don't have to be afraid. At Christmas time, we let in light and banish shade. And in your world of plenty, we can spread a smile of joy. Throw your arms around the world at Christmas time.' And then it goes, 'But say a prayer, at Christmas time it's hard, but when you're having fun, there's a world outside your window, it's a world of dread and fear . . .'.

SKINNER: **You're recording it tomorrow, with this twenty-odd number of acts in it. It's going to be mayhem, isn't it?**

GELDOF: No, I don't think so. At the end of the song, it goes into the sort of classic John Lennon chant type of thing, and the words will be 'Feed the world, let them know it's Christmas.' That's mainly what we want everybody there for.

SKINNER: **When does the record hit the shops?**

GELDOF: December third it'll be in the shops. We start it tomorrow, and a week from now it'll actually be in the shops.

SKINNER: **And the band are called Band Aid?**

GELDOF: Yes.

SKINNER: **Look forward to hearing it.**

The following day, 25 November 1984, Radio 1's Newsbeat *managed to snatch a few words with Bob at the recording studio, where he bluntly explained why he was there.*

GELDOF: Everybody has felt impotent and enraged and disgusted by what is going on, and I think that if we don't do something, we're participants in a vast human crime.

The next day, the finished track was rushed to Radio 1 for its first airing on the Simon Bates Show, *and two weeks later 'Do They Know It's Christmas?' was Number One. On 11 December, Bob spoke again to* Newsbeat, *when Frank Partridge asked him about topping the charts.*

GELDOF: I'm delighted. And exhausted. I think that the whole spirit of the thing has precisely caught the atmosphere of Christmas. I think that in retrospect, we didn't anticipate that. The idea of Band Aid is the important thing. No body actually exists as Band Aid, except the Band Aid Trust. People enjoy that idea, and with a million people going out and buying it, they've obviously taken to it, and they're as much a part of it as the actual band members themselves. I think the important thing today, in amongst all the euphoria, is to thank everybody who went out to buy it. I've been hearing amazing stories all week — of people buying fifty copies and giving back forty-nine to the stores to resell. All those things are phenomenal. But in amongst that, I have to remind people to please keep going out and buying it. Because every one is someone saved. It's wonderful and it's an amazing achievement to have the fastest-selling record ever in Britain. But we must keep on, and see if we can make it three million, which isn't difficult with fifty-two million people in Britain. That should be the goal. And if you're having trouble getting it — which is what's happening in a lot of shops . . . because all the pressing plants in Britain are pressing the record, every one of them, including CBS and EMI and Phonogram, we've now gone to, I think, twenty pressing plants on the Continent to press up the record, and still there isn't enough to fulfil the orders — so if you're having trouble, please, keep going back, don't get frustrated. Make the commitment that you're going to have to go to a lot of trouble to get it. But it will be worth it.

PARTRIDGE: We hear there's enormous interest in the United States as well.

GELDOF: Yes, it went out yesterday on general release, and they've printed six million.

PARTRIDGE: What about the money itself? How long is it going to take to get all the proceeds in, and then get it back out again to Ethiopia?

GELDOF: Usually it takes about a year or six months to get proceeds in from any record. But because nobody's getting paid on this record, it'll just come straight into the record companies and straight to the Band Aid account. It looks like the total amount raised by this one song will exceed the total UNICEF budget for 1985 in that part of Africa. And the nice thing about 'Do They Know It's Christmas?' is that this week, and hopefully over Christmas, practically every one of the great rock bands in the world are Number One at the same time. I think they're very excited by it. They think of it as their own record, which it is. I'd like to thank them all for it, and say, 'Well done, lads, you've got another Number One.' Brilliant.

In January 1985 Bob went to America, to a press conference to launch Band Aid's US counterpart, USA For Africa, featuring Michael Jackson, Stevie Wonder, Diana Ross, Paul Simon, Bruce Springsteen, Bob Dylan, Ray Charles and many others. Radio 1's Newsbeat was there, and found Bob as outspoken as ever.

GELDOF: Certainly this famine, which potentially will kill a hundred million people, is one of the great shameful things of our time. I find it an indictment of us, and a pathetic way of living, that a piece of plastic, seven inches across with a hole in the middle, is the price of someone's life this year.

By July, the stars were lining up again, on both sides of the Atlantic. This time for Live Aid, a sixteen-hour, transglobal extravaganza of live music. It's 13 July 1985, and Radio 1's Janice Long is backstage at London's Wembley Stadium.

LONG: **Bob, you were standing in the Royal Box – I was watching you, on a monitor – when they began the whole event. How did it feel for you, the culmination of all your hard work?**

GELDOF: Everybody was crying around me. I just thought, 'Christ, what a noise!' I think then the scale of the thing hit me, when I saw all those people. And the atmosphere of the thing is not like any other rock gig I've been to.

LONG: **The concert has come together in a relatively short time, hasn't it?**

GELDOF: Yes, about four months.

LONG: **How do you hope that the money is going to be used? What are your priorities now?**

GELDOF: Keeping people alive, still. Not only now, but in the long term as well. . . . I just want to say hello to everyone in Australia, because they've been going for a few hours now, and I keep listening to what's going on there, and it's brilliant. Good luck to you all down there, and thanks for helping.

LONG: Is it grain or is it transport that this money is going to be spent on?

GELDOF: Oh, everything, including wells, planting trees, transport, medicine, shelter . . . I'm off. . . .

LONG: I know, you've got to go on stage. . . .

JANICE LONG CATCHES BOB GELDOF BACKSTAGE AT LIVE AID JUST BEFORE HE PERFORMS

But Janice did get the chance for a fuller discussion with Bob in January 1986, in the less fraught surroundings of the Radio 1 studios, for a phone-in which allowed listeners to ask Geldof directly about where the money was going.

LONG: **We can actually go to the lines now. Alison Lynham is in Birmingham.**

CALLER: I've got all the records and the T-shirt, and I've bought all the books that have been published. I wondered if there is anything else I can do to help.

GELDOF: You're doing brilliantly. What you can do to help is to keep it uppermost in your mind. It isn't last year's thing. This is the New Year, but it means nothing to people who are dying. What you can really do is . . . you seem to understand exactly what it's all about, but don't let your friends forget. If there's anything possible you can do at school or at work, please do, because just before we came in here we got messages from the west of Sudan, which apparently looks exactly like what Ethiopia looked when we first saw those films. It looks like all the big government donors like the EEC and the US and the western world in general are not committing themselves to help these people this year. Which means that by October next year, we're going to see the same horrific scenes. You have been warned now. And the governments have been warned, and if they refuse to act then, without doubt, they're going to be guilty of murder. Obviously, you are going to act and do whatever you can, so good luck with it, and keep doing whatever you can.

LONG: **Isobel Smith is next, in Hastings. Hello, Isobel.**

CALLER: Hi. I was thinking about what an enormous task you've committed yourself to, and it's been going on for so long already. Do you think that it's become so much a part of your life that you won't be able to detach yourself from it?

GELDOF: I think I've done everything that I can do. The point of Band Aid was to raise the issue, and then the money that came in after we raised the issue we set out to spend. Once we had Live Aid, we'd created literally a global constituency of compassion, and that became a political instrument. I went to the political capitals of the world using only that constituency, and saying, 'Look, 50 per cent of the world's population actually do care. Now the obligation is yours to do something.' We got a lot of things out of it. I think by and large Band Aid money was extended to double its amount just by deals we did with those people. That's the most that I can personally do. With regard to the people who work in Band Aid, they have committed themselves to it and to spending that money as best as possible. But I don't ever want it to become an institution. I don't want it to become like Oxfam or Save the Children, because they'll be there long after we've gone. We can't compete with them. They're the ones who do the work. I think that the main point was proven that individuals can make a difference, that people do care, and really governments ignore that at their peril.

LONG: **Now we go to Melanie Pellet, who's next. Melanie is in Basingstoke.**

CALLER: Do you think that by the time the Band Aid Trust closes at the end of the year, the situation will have been sufficiently remedied for no more money-raising to be necessary?

GELDOF: I don't know, Melanie. If we're able to close at the end of the year, we'll close at the end of the year. If there's further work for us to do, then we'll do it. But I really think that our 'mission', if you like, will have been completed by then. We will be doing, I think, hopefully Sports Aid this year, and there may be one or two other things. Like there's Hearing Aid, which is the Heavy Metal thing. Despite what people tell you, the money is absolutely crucial because it allows the aid agencies to continue to do their work. Band Aid will spend the money that people gave it, and hopefully then it will be able to close its doors and say, 'Look, once in your life it was possible, and it was incorruptible, and it *did* work, and it was generally good,' and I think that will be enough for us to have done. But I don't think the work that we are talking about will be in any way complete. I think that you have to go on supporting the Oxfams, the Save the Childrens, the UNICEFs.

LONG: To the Wirral next. It's David Pollard. What are your feelings, David?

CALLER: Don't you think it's bizarre that a rock star from Dublin should stand up and say, 'No more', and that the whole Live Aid thing has exposed this and every other government's lack of aid and the lack of interest in Africa and the Third World?

GELDOF: I do think it's pathetic that it was down to pop singers. But then again, I didn't expect it to be such a fuss, you know. Once it had happened, I was kind of left holding the baby. But I think that it took most governments really by surprise.

....

BOB GELDOF IN ETHIOPIA – 'INDIVIDUALS CAN MAKE A DIFFERENCE, PEOPLE DO CARE,
AND GOVERNMENTS IGNORE THAT AT THEIR PERIL'

That was the great thing about it. They were really shocked by it. I really wouldn't have been able to stroll up the steps of Capitol Hill—

CALLER: [INTERRUPTING] What would have happened if you hadn't been the catalyst for it? There wouldn't have been Band Aid, there wouldn't have been Live Aid, there wouldn't have been the T-shirts. I mean, what would have happened?

GELDOF: Erm . . . I don't know.

LONG: **Bob, you're saying you want to wind things up. Do you think that life will ever be the same for you?**

GELDOF: No. Quite evidently, it's the single most important thing I've ever done in my life. I don't think I'll ever be able to wind it up, that's not my intent. My intent is not to do any more PR stuff. Not to have to comment on every dot and full stop and capital letter in everything that Band Aid does. I'll remain as chairman of the Board of Trustees. I'll go down to the office a couple of days a week. But I think the main job is for me to be the sort of . . . almost the moral fervour, the hysterical one behind the whole thing. Beyond that, I don't know what else there is to do, so it's a question of being able now to pull back and get on with the remainder of my life. But I'm not pulling out. I will always remember 1985 as being an extraordinary time.

MARK KNOPFLER

SATURDAY LIVE was Radio 1's new rock magazine programme in 1985. On 4 May, Andy Batten-Foster spoke to Mark Knopfler about Dire Straits and about the forthcoming album Brothers in Arms. The producer was Mark Radcliffe.

'I knew Knopfler didn't like doing interviews,' remembers Andy, 'but I knew it had to happen because we'd been given the first play of Brothers in Arms anywhere in the world. I went to Paris two days early to meet up with him and try to get to know him a bit. For the twenty-four hours before the interview was scheduled, we kind of circled each other, talking about everything but music. Eventually, we just said, "OK, let's get it over with." Although he hates talking about his work, he did loosen up, and we got about an hour on tape. The thing that came through for me was that here was a man who lived only for performing. What drove him was the joy of playing live.

'Dire Straits were already quite big at the time, but hearing Brothers in Arms for the first time on the plane going over to Paris, I knew it was something special. It had a much richer, deeper feel than their previous stuff. I think I was the first person outside the band and the record company to hear that famous opening riff of "Money for Nothing" — and it was immediately obvious as a classic.'

BROTHERS IN ARMS – 'IT'S SORT OF PINK AND BLUE, AND THERE'S A GUITAR ON THE FRONT'

BATTEN-FOSTER: **You've never really been a band who've followed fashion, have you?**

KNOPFLER: We are, I think, probably more concerned about the quality of the music and the lasting quality and the style of the music rather than this week's trousers, definitely.

BATTEN-FOSTER: **But I mean fashion in terms of sounds as well, really.**

KNOPFLER: Well, I mean, I mean that too. That's never really made any sense to me anyway. I think this whole thing about waves, styles, approaches and things like that has been for the convenience of broadcasters. To me it doesn't really make any sense. Songs to me have always been just individual expression at different times. I don't particularly see things in terms of this is 'techno-pop', this is this, this is that.

BATTEN-FOSTER: **Let's play a track that I really love, an out-and-out love song it seems to me, 'Why Worry'. Can you talk about this a bit?**

KNOPFLER: Well, I'm not altogether sure why I write these little things [LAUGHS]. I suppose . . . it's nice to maybe do something that you feel people can use for themselves as well as just satisfying your own situation or whatever.

BATTEN-FOSTER: **How do you mean?**

KNOPFLER: It's just nice when people come and that, and they tell you about what a song is for them, then that reality is just as valid as it is for you.

BATTEN-FOSTER: **Even if it has nothing to do with the ideas that you had when you were writing it?**

KNOPFLER: Yeah . . . even if it really is not that connected. It's good. You realise in those situations that there are some redeeming qualities in what you do, you know that you're actually giving people some positive things.

BATTEN-FOSTER: **We're playing 'Walk of Life' from the *Brothers in Arms* album — we're talking to Mark Knopfler. Because the terrible thing about listening to an album at this stage, very very advanced, is I can't see the whole package. I mean, for example, the cover, things like that. How much work do you put into those?**

KNOPFLER: Not a lot, really. It's all been done. We sort of monitor these things as they go along.

BATTEN-FOSTER: **So what's it going to look like? That's what I'm really asking. What's the album gonna actually look like?**

KNOPFLER: Sort of pink and blue and there's a guitar on the front.

BATTEN-FOSTER: Oh, that's a nice change, isn't it? [LAUGHS]

KNOPFLER: There's a guitar on the back, too. And there's gonna be lyrics inside it for people in Europe.

BATTEN-FOSTER: Are these important? Because I've been trying to listen to it without lyrics, and it's funny, people still really want to sit down and listen to the album and read the lyric sheet at the same time.

....

MARK KNOPFLER IN 1985 – 'WHAT DROVE HIM WAS THE JOY OF PLAYING LIVE'

KNOPFLER: Oh yeah they do, they listen to it and screw their eyes up and try and figure out what it's all about.

BATTEN-FOSTER: Didn't you use to do exactly the same, though?

KNOPFLER: Yeah. Oh yeah. Yeah. And it's very important for a lot of the kids who can't speak English. If you don't do that then they write in and want lyrics.

BATTEN-FOSTER: What, you've actually had requests, have you, for things?

KNOPFLER: Yeah, I left it off the second album — I thought, 'What's all this about?' and left it off, and of course the result was that people went nuts about not having the lyrics. Lyrics are very important to a lot of people. They like to read them. So you do have to put them in. Of course Japan I can't really speak about, because they do their own translations over there and they're just so out to lunch, it's the biggest joke. . . .

BATTEN-FOSTER: What, do they get it wrong?

KNOPFLER: That's an understatement, yeah.

BATTEN-FOSTER: I think we're very lucky, I think both of us are very lucky inasmuch as we're doing something and getting paid for what we would do for free.

KNOPFLER: Yeah, I don't think there's any argument about that. I think what is important is to eventually find the thing . . . it might take a while. It certainly took me a while and I did dozens and dozens of other jobs, but I think I always wanted to do this and now I'm doing it. That's it to me. I think it's most important for a kid to do what he or she wants to do. There's no substitute for that. Most people get in the situation where they don't necessarily look forward to much. Sometimes it's to the weekend, or whatever. But there's something very special about waking up in the morning and looking forward to the next day, or this day. I think you're doing all right if you can just look forward to that. I think you're doing a lot better than the vast majority of people. But working is very important. It's very important to just enjoy that work vibe and just to be getting up and having something to do. Which is why unemployment is such a serious matter just in terms of what it does to people's sense of themselves, sense of who they are. Also, another thing is that your old lady kicks you out the house. . . . If you're just hanging around there, you just start getting on people's nerves. It's important to have something to go out and do rather than just being thrown out, you know.

BATTEN-FOSTER: It's something you came close to touching on with 'Industrial Disease' on the last album, this business of everybody being wound down and there not being the motivation, the work for people to do. Are you never tempted to make stronger statements as far as that's concerned, political statements?

KNOPFLER: Well, I think everybody is political in some ways. When I think about working with music, I don't necessarily think about grand schemes and big themes, although it may well end up that way. What I was talking about before about the level of different meanings that you can take songs at and the ripple effect of the music and how it's used and perceived generally — if it is sensitising people, then it's doing its thing. I mean I want it to work as of itself. I don't want it to have some kind of crutch or some kind of flag flying above it which will detract from its ability to stand on its own foundations as a piece of work.

BATTEN-FOSTER: Is that again because you think that what you do best is make points in a different way or. . . .

KNOPFLER: I think that's partly . . . that's partly it. But there's ways of making points.

BATTEN-FOSTER: But don't you sometimes get angry enough to stand up and shout something as well?

KNOPFLER: Well, it depends where, when, why, what . . . it's such a complicated thing. I mean, I'm very mistrustful of organisations of anything. I don't really like badges. I'm not a believer in politicians or political parties as such, or that kind of thing. I have a sort of an inbuilt mistrust of institutionalised things like that. My actual philosophy is probably more, everybody should leave everybody else alone and it would be a much better world, a much better place to live in if there was some kind of check built into that sort of natural propensity that people have to interfere in other people's lives. That's the way I feel generally about most things.

DIRE STRAITS ★ 1985

SINGLES	REACHED
So Far Away	UK No. 20
Money for Nothing	UK No. 4
Money for Nothing	US No. 1
Brothers in Arms	UK No. 16
Walk of Life	US No. 13
(later No. 7 in Jan 1986)	

ALBUMS	REACHED
Brothers in Arms	UK No. 1
Brothers in Arms	US No. 1

1986

JOHN PEEL

RADIO, RADIO, produced by Kevin Howlett, was a 1986 series profiling six of the great Radio 1 DJs, men who had made a unique contribution to the history of the station. The interviews were conducted by Tim Blackmore:

'I chaired the 1985 Radio Academy conference, where Paul Gambaccini gave the opening address, on the subject of "Radio Ga Ga". Paul's speech was a spellbinding account of his love of radio, from his early days as a listener and music fan to his work as a practitioner of the medium. In a discussion afterwards with Radio 1's Controller, Johnny Beerling, and producer Kevin Howlett, we decided that the speech could be the basis of a wonderful programme, which then developed into the idea of doing a whole series on the most important British music presenters over the years.

'John Peel was, of course, one of the six we chose for the series. Despite his reputation as a maverick, John went on to become the only Radio 1 DJ to work continually for the station throughout its first twenty-five years.

'Although he had honed his craft as part of mainstream radio in America in the sixties, in the UK he's uniquely been his own man rather than being the mouthpiece for a particular format. Through his love and understanding of music, and his constant thirst for that which is new and different — and, one has to add, through the indulgence of the BBC — John has made an immeasurable contribution to popular music. He's supported literally thousands of new bands, and has provided the first foothold for trends ranging from punk to reggae, to rap and hip-hop. The other ingredient which makes his programme compulsive listening is John's totally seductive sense of humour — something which also pervaded our interview for Radio, Radio, which was broadcast as John telling his own story, with my questions edited out.'

PEEL: I didn't become aware of listening to the radio deliberately until I started listening to Radio Luxembourg and the American Forces Network [AFN] when I was about ten or eleven years old. Then I heard Elvis Presley on *Two-Way Family Favourites* with 'Heartbreak Hotel'. I'd read a little bit in the music press about Elvis Presley, but nothing had prepared me for the reality of it. Just the starkness of it was one of those things which was quite literally transcendental. Something which my children will never experience, because they've grown up very gradually with all of popular music, and I don't think there's going to be one of those things that's called something like a 'quantum jump' of anything that's going to be so radically different.

DJ JOHN PEEL IN 1968 – 'I WAS JUST MYSELF – NAÏVE AND HOPELESS'

So I heard Elvis, and then on AFN a week or so later I heard Little Richard. I would say hearing Little Richard on AFN was like Saul on the road to Damascus. Genuinely, nothing was ever the same again.

I think at some stage I wrote to the BBC. My father warned me against the BBC, because he said unless I was a homosexual or a Roman Catholic I'd never get a job on the station. As I was neither, it seemed to me that I was rather wasting my time. But I wrote to Pete Murray, I think, and asked him the traditional, 'How do you get on the radio?' He didn't write back, so I rather abandoned the idea of trying to get on the radio, because it did seem to me quite impossible. There were no regional stations, and very few disc jockeys anyway.

During National Service, I at least had the opportunity for the first time to play records that I liked to at least a room full of other people. They all thought I was a complete twerp, of course, and probably quite rightly so, but we used to have Little Richard recitals in the billet. I'd got the only record-player in our battery, so people, almost because there was no other entertainment, used to come in and

I used to play them these records.

At the end of National Service, my father said he'd send me to America. Initially, my reaction was, 'OK, send me, see if I care.' But it did occur to me at the time that there might be a possibility that because of my Englishness I might be able to wangle my way on to a radio station over there where they might regard me as a bit of a novelty.

I was entranced by the radio over there. There were two competing Top Forty stations in Dallas — KILF and K-BOX Tiger Radio. You almost wanted to listen to them both at the same time; it was exciting, because anything that you ever wanted was on there. Within half an hour, any record that you wanted to hear would appear.

The really hip programme was one on station WRR called *Kat's Karavan*, from ten o'clock till midnight, oddly enough the hours that I broadcast on Radio 1 at the moment. It was basically R&B stuff. It always struck me that the people who I knew at the time who listened to these programmes, and who bought Jimmy Reed records and who went to see Jimmy Reed play in places like the High Hope Ballroom, if he had turned up on their doorstep their parents would probably have set the dogs on him.

During my National Service, I'd been acquiring some obscure blues records, so I took these down to the radio station. To my amazement, quite clearly the people who listened to Jimmy Reed records, and even the people who were doing the programme, had no real idea of the history of the blues. So they were quite amazed to hear these records, because not only were they not available to an American audience, but nobody had ever heard them. So I took them in and said, 'Would you be interested in playing these?', and they said, 'Yes, very much so.' I went to sit in the studio while they were playing them, and then the DJ, Hoss Carroll, said, 'Let's talk to the man who's loaned them to us', so they put me on the radio. I think part of the reason they put me on was because I must have sounded so bizarre. I sounded like a minor member of the Royal Family, very, very nasal, very high pitched, and talking the most appalling codswallop.

After this, they allowed me to have an hour on the radio every Monday evening, unpaid. Anyway, I was listening to KILF, Russ Knight, the Weird Beard, and he was talking about Liverpool, because the Beatles were just becoming voguish. He was talking incredible nonsense because he knew nothing about it. I phoned them up and said, 'Really you're talking a load of rubbish here', and they said, 'Are you from Liverpool?' and I said, 'Yes', because as far as Americans need know, I was, although actually I was from the other side of the river. So on the strength of having an approximation of a Liverpool accent, I became a surrogate Beatle in Dallas. I used to get mobbed. For three or four nights in a row, the Weird Beard used to phone me up for a bit of a chat about Liverpool and about the Beatles — of course about whom I knew nothing at all. I was having to invent a lot of it. People were phoning up and saying, 'Hey, what colour are Paul McCartney's eyes?' and crucial stuff like this, and I had no idea at all. So as soon as the first Beatles books appeared, I had to whizz out and buy them and memorise them. Of course, they tended to be full of conflicting information. It was all very confusing. I had to work very hard.

After a while of being the Beatle man at the other end of the phone, they asked me if I'd appear at a store in Dallas with the Weird Beard to give away some Beatles LPs. We were actually met on the way to the store by a terrified manager, because instead of the 100 or so girls that they'd expected, they'd got about 3000. At that time, I was looking like a minor member of the Kennedy clan — very collegiate, not at all Beatley. I got up on to this small platform and Russ Knight said, 'Here's our man from Liverpool', to faint screams and so on. Then he asked me how long I'd been in America. At the time, I'd been there four and a half years, so as soon as I said 'harf', instead of 'hy-aff', they just became completely unstitched. It was a riot. Really, girls being sick, girls fainting, girls screaming, 'Touch me!' (which, of course, I was only too happy to do). It was just Beatlemania, or Ravenscroft mania, as I was at the time. We actually had to be spirited out of the store. I'm not sure whether it was in a laundry van or not, but I like to imagine that it might have been. And from then on I was a celebrity.

On the back of his fame, John worked on stations in Dallas, Oklahoma and California. By the time he got a job with K-MEN in San Bernadino, he was a highly prized DJ.

I went straight on to the morning programme there. I was out every night. I used to go into Los Angeles and see bands: people like Love, the Doors and Captain Beefheart. At the weekend, instead of doing a three-hour shift, seven days, you did a six-hour shift, either on Saturday or Sunday. Because I was the top DJ in the market at the time, I was allowed a certain amount of flexibility with this. I used to play LP tracks, which was unheard-of at the time. I also used to present a rigged British chart, where all kind of records, like 'The Naz is Blue' by The Yardbirds, used to mysteriously appear in my English chart, which I used to say I'd got from an unimpeachable source in Liverpool. It was a ludicrous story, which they were quite happy to accept.

Early in 1967, I was married at the time to an American girl. She was a girl: we got married when she was fifteen. It was a fairly catastrophic marriage, so I decided to get out to the extent of coming back to Britain. Obviously, I had no work, and no expectation of work. A fellow who was living next to me at the time had dealings with Radio London, the pirate ship, and he said why didn't I go along and see Alan Keen, who was running the station from the offices in Curzon Street. So I went along. Fortunately, they didn't ask me to audition. They were sufficiently impressed by the fact that I'd been working on the radio in California to give me a job.

I went out on to the ship, and as the junior member of the team, I had to do two programmes. There was a daytime programme, which was the regular Radio London fare, and also a late-night programme from twelve till two. Initially, I just used to do this as I had done the other programme — run commercials and do the weather and the news and all the other things I was supposed to do. Gradually it dawned on me that nobody was actually listening to this programme, I mean nobody in the Radio London office, and certainly nobody on the ship. So I started to improvise a little bit, and gradually stopped running the ads and so on, and playing more of this music that I'd brought back from America with me, and also adding a British dimension, with people like The Incredible String Band, and Hendrix, and Pink Floyd and Tyrannosaurus Rex, all these sort of people. I called the programme *The Perfumed Garden*. By the time I got round to calling it that, I'd entirely dispensed with the format. I was reading people's poetry, extraordinarily badly. People were writing poetry and sending it in. It was the Summer of Love, and it became compulsive listening for anybody who was into that. This was all over Northern Europe. In fact, I still encounter people in Holland when I go over there who remember it, which is quite nice. The first inkling that Alan Keen had that this was going on, so legend has it, was when Brian Epstein phoned him up to congratulate him on having had the foresight to put such a programme out. Of course, he listened and was horrified. But by this time Radio London had only got a few months left anyway [because pirate radio was about to become illegal] so they decided that they might as well leave things as they were.

The BBC when they established Radio 1 were compelled to take on DJs from the pirate stations. They had no choice, really. I applied along with all of the others. I think there must have been more than a little reluctance for them to give me work, but they were aware of the success of *The Perfumed Garden*, even if they didn't like it. This is one of the things that the BBC was doing then, and has done ever since, really. One of the things which I find admirable is even if the people who run the station don't actually like what you do, they can see that there is a justification for it. Nobody's ever interfered with the content of the programme at all.

I've always admired natural broadcasters, so I was quite pleased to be myself really, not to have to do a kind of Top Forty voice, or an American voice, or a slightly Liverpool voice, or whatever I'd been required to do in the past. I was just myself, naïve and hopeless, but not projecting myself in any way at all, just talking in my ordinary voice as I'm speaking to you now. At the time it was seen as a radical departure, but to me it seems like a logical thing to do. It seems to me also an easy thing to do.

On the radio, brevity is of the essence really, so I try and say as little as possible. The letters that people send in to the programme are crucially important. It's impossible to answer all of them, but at least they all get read. They tend to be fairly thoughtful letters, quite amusing letters in some cases, from people who picked up something that you've said or on some record and want to know more, and will occasionally recommend something to you. The thing that I like best is when people go away on their holidays, they send me postcards. They sit down and write postcards to their mates at home and to their mum and dad, and then they'll send me one. But the relationship for me is actually like a mate. I regard myself as the fan's man on the inside. It's my job to find interesting stuff and stick it out on the radio with a minimum of fuss.

I think my role is an editorial one, rather than a presenting one, because the bulk of my energies goes into finding material to put on the programme. Finding bands who we can get in to record sessions . . . you can get bands in who've not yet

PEEL IN 1986 – 'I REGARD MYSELF AS THE FANS' MAN ON THE INSIDE'

recorded, or you can get combinations of musicians in who may never record, or get big bands to come in to do a kind of 'work in progress' session, which I think is excellent. I'm quite often presented in the papers as being a kind of taste-maker and a moulder of public appetite, but I really don't believe that at all. If people are any good, they're going to become public property eventually anyway, so all you can do is either accelerate or retard the process.

We kept Bowie alive for a couple of years. He went through a bad patch of not getting very much work, and people not paying a great deal of attention to him. He did a lot of sessions during that time. And Tyrannosaurus Rex, I suppose. It's one of those things where you become aware of the destructive nature of notoriety and fame. It's one of those areas that occasionally bothers me about what I do – when you take quite innocent, enthusiastic people out of their natural milieu you can easily be creating monsters. There have been people in bands that I've endorsed who've subsequently died as a result of the rock 'n' roll lifestyle, and there are times when you feel quite guilty about that. But I think if you stop and examine what you do in that much detail, that way lies madness, frankly.

Being in a position to recommend bands for sessions, and to see them subsequently go on to become notorious, or to disappear without trace, it doesn't really matter – in a way, it's almost like a classic seventeenth-century role, in that you can be a patron of the arts, with the unique and gratifying difference that you don't have to invest any of your own money in it. But this is something that the BBC has traditionally done, so I feel that, in a way, the thinking behind the programme, if there is any thinking, is more in the Reithian tradition than a lot of other stuff that goes on in the rest of the BBC.

My producer, John Walters, once said that the programme would be in real trouble if I ever reached puberty. Obviously, my enthusiasms, on the surface anyway, would seem to be those of a thirteen or fourteen-year-old, in that you're always looking for something new, and never entirely satisfied with what you've got. But on the other hand, it's only in the area of popular music that this is seen as the way things should be. In other areas of artistic appreciation, the idea that your appreciation diminishes with age is just not on. In fact, it seems to be enhanced with the passage of time – until you become senile, of course. I always find that football provides quite a useful metaphor for most things in life, so I relate things to football; so I'd say in the same way that I'm more concerned about what Liverpool do next Saturday, or next season, than what they did last Saturday or in their long and glorious history. It's the same with the music. I'm more interested in the records that I've not yet heard, that I've got in the back of the car to listen to at the weekend, than I am in the ones I've already played in this week's programme. When the time comes when I lose my enthusiasm, or there's some major development and I feel

I don't feel involved with it or it's nothing to do with me, then that's when I'd have to — I couldn't fake it, after all these years — that's when I'd have to shut up shop and say, 'Well, from now on, my period is from 1948 to whenever it happens to be, from now on I'm a museum.' If that were the case, I hope that as a museum I'd continue to find some function, because I like doing radio programmes. I've no ambition beyond that. That's why I quite like doing television, because it genuinely doesn't matter to me if they say, 'You're never going to do television again'. That wouldn't bother me. So when I do television, I don't see it as being a springboard to a career as a TV quizmaster or something, because I don't want to do that. What I want to do is radio programmes — with a bit of writing, I like writing — but the radio is what I do, and what I want to do.

PEEL AND LONG-TIME RADIO 1 PRODUCER JOHN WALTERS, WHO ADMITTED 'THE PROGRAMME
WOULD BE IN REAL TROUBLE IF PEEL EVER REACHED PUBERTY'

1987

ERIC CLAPTON

BEHIND THE MASK seemed doubly appropriate as the title of Radio 1's 1987 six-part series on Eric Clapton. Not only was it the name of his first Top Twenty single in twelve years, it also summed up the style of this in-depth look at Clapton's life and career. His comeback with this single, and with the parent album August, proved that 'God' was playing better than ever. The series marking this Indian summer in his career was ideally timed – a tribute both to his virtuosity and his longevity.

As soon as producer Roger Lewis received the agreement of Clapton's manager, Roger Forrester, to do the series, a galaxy of stars came forward to offer contributions, including George Harrison, Elton John and Phil Collins. However, it was a two-hour interview with Radio 1's Simon Bates which proved the key to the programmes. Face to face at Forrester's house on 6 February 1987, Clapton was frank and relaxed as they talked, stage by stage, through his career, and about the recurring themes of his life – his love for the blues, his lapses into dependency on drugs and alcohol – and about his new-found contentment.

CLAPTON IS PRESENTED WITH A *RADIO TIMES* COVER MARKING THE *BEHIND THE MASK* SERIES BY RADIO 1'S JOHNNY BEERLING AND ROGER LEWIS (LEFT) AND BBC DIRECTOR GENERAL, MICHAEL CHECKLAND

BATES: **Now, you came from a Surrey background: people who were 1950s people and therefore probably didn't listen to the radio very much. So where did music come from?**

CLAPTON: Uncle Mac's radio show [*Children's Favourites*]. Remember Uncle Mac? I can literally remember him playing a Chuck Berry record. I remember him playing 'Memphis Tennessee' when it first came out. It just went straight in and nailed me to the wall and I listened regularly to see if he'd chuck anything else in. I can remember that very programme when he played 'Memphis Tennessee'. I suppose I was about eleven or twelve. I just kept my ears open and I started to get a kind of input of whatever R&B and rock 'n' roll was going to be played, things like 'Hound Dog' when that first came out. A couple of kids and me, we were still fourteen, fifteen, we'd rush off and play it, lock ourselves in the parents' front room, get the record-player out. It was all like breaking the law, very kind of illicit, to listen to this music.

BATES: **Can you remember your first musical instrument?**

CLAPTON: Yeah. An acoustic guitar on the HP from Bell's of Surbiton. I was trying to play like Buddy Holly first of all. Much as I loved the Shadows and what they did for the English music scene, I always went for what I thought was the real thing, which came from across the ocean. So Buddy Holly was the first rock 'n' roll thing. Then I wanted to try and play like Big Bill Broonzy. It's a phenomenon that I can't explain, but it hit me like a ton of bricks and I *had* to go out then to a record shop and find anything by Big Bill Broonzy. When I found it, I put it on the record-player and it was *exactly* what I thought it would be, and better. So then I would try and play like that. And then you'd turn the album cover over and you'd read on the back in French — it'd be a French RCA album or something — but you'd see other names like Leadbelly, or whoever his contemporaries were. So then you'd go and buy their records and sooner or later you were involved in this massive kind of scholarship of the blues and R&B — and that became my quest.

BATES: **Let me ask you — someone I was talking to said you were very serious as a teenager. Were you?**

CLAPTON: Very boring, yeah. Very serious and totally dogmatic, from that point of having discovered these things for myself, really. All of my musical study from that point on was done on my own. I really would get into heated arguments about who was playing harmonica on a record. I knew, I literally did know nine times out of ten. You know, you get the real blues purists. We'd have meetings and we'd listen to a record and say, 'Who is that playing the second guitar on that Little Walter record?' And I'd go, 'Well, it's Jimmie Rodgers,' and they'd say, 'Well, it's Pat Hare.' And no one would ever be able to prove it. But I always knew I was right. So I became very, very defensive. That's why I was serious. I was very defensive of what I thought was my cause in life, which was to protect and further this beautiful form of music. And I knew better than anyone how it was made, the character of the people that were making it and what they lived like.

BATES: **Looking back on it now, as we sit in 1987, what is the blues to you?**

CLAPTON: Ah! For the most part, it's a dying art form which really needs a lot of energy pumped back into it. I still hold that as being my main purpose. I don't talk about it like we're talking about it here very much, and I don't really listen to it as much any more as I used to, but I hold it in my playing and in the way I play. Also the way I sing, I guess, is completely derived from the blues. I think it's the main root basically of what rock 'n' roll is. You know rock 'n' roll isn't based on jazz, it's not based on classical music, it's based on the blues. And any good R&B or rock singer, like from Stevie Wonder to Ray Charles to George Michael, has to have that feeling. Even if you don't know where it comes from, you have to have that feeling. The difference with me was that I was vastly curious and had to know what it was all about, which is why I went back and back and back and found out about it all. But it's still there even in people who aren't really aware of why they sing like that. If they have that feeling, it's come from the blues.

BATES: **You were soon playing around the music scene and you had some success with The Yardbirds, but . . .**

CLAPTON: I did the famous walkout of The Yardbirds. I made small pop history there and I shook myself up a bit in doing it.

BATES: **Why did you walk out?**

CLAPTON: Because I saw success coming up. Tinsel Town was on the horizon. There was an obvious Top Ten hit ['For Your Love'] being performed by the group. Giorgio Gomelsky was lining us up with TV appearances here and there, you know, *Thank Your Lucky Stars* and *Top of the Pops*, and I didn't give a damn for all that. I just wanted to play this music. The other guys were more easygoing about it. Maybe they would keep the act as long as they could, you know, make their hits. Well, I just was completely dogmatic about it so I said, 'No, I'm leaving.'

BATES: **And John Mayall stands up.**

CLAPTON: John Mayall's Bluesbreakers was the first serious band that I came up against. I'd gone off to see Ben Palmer, who used to be in a band called The Roosters with me, to try and talk him into forming a blues band or making a record of blues, or whatever. But he didn't want to, he was into something else. He put me up for a while. I was staying up with him in Oxford for about a month, and I got a phone call from John Mayall, who said would I care to come and meet him and talk about playing in the band? I thought, 'Yeah', and then I went out and bought a John Mayall album. I thought, 'Well, this is a bit jazzy', but actually I felt that I could introduce something into that situation to make it really good. And when I did meet John and I took one look at his record collection, I knew I was home — because he had it all. He offered to put me up, so I lived in his house and I went through his record collection and that's when I really honed it. I really . . . I went to school, I went to graduation school as it were, in terms of what I wanted to do and how to play what I knew I wanted to play. I'd just stay in this little room that I was living in in his house and I'd go through his record collection and get my guitar out and I'd play all day. I'd learn everything I could. And that went on for a couple of years.

BATES: **You said you were into reality and yet you stomped out on John Mayall. That would seem to be, as a career decision, the wrong thing to do.**

CLAPTON: And yet I don't think it was. I don't regret it. What was happening with John was that we were becoming academics. We were becoming what I'd wanted the Yardbirds to be, which was to be an academic blues band which does it exactly by the book and with a little bit of theatrics thrown in — you know, John would take his shirt off or something. But basically, it was dying, it was getting stale for me and I wanted to actually keep the blues alive but put it in some kind of new contemporary setting, instead of playing like the records all the time. And then I met Ginger [Baker] and I felt this kind of fire from him and Jack [Bruce]. In terms of their jazz improvisation, they were forward-thinking musicians. That really caught light for me. That just swept me off my feet. I realised that there was something more than just doing it by the book. I fell in love with Ginger's fire and his irreverence towards everything. And that was it.

BATES: **So were you the person who was . . . the architect, if you like, of setting Cream up?**

CLAPTON: I think I was the middle man, Ginger was the architect. He was the one that had the dream about getting me and then getting some other musicians, but Jack was the one person he didn't want. [LAUGHS] And so from the word go, the group was really doomed. From the first rehearsal we had a flaming row between Jack and Ginger. But they loved one another at the same time, a real love–hate relationship, which I somehow managed to get stuck in the middle of.

BATES: **How did it survive, though, from that very bad beginning?**

CLAPTON: I think success, the success of it. I mean, instant success. The first gig we played we only had like a half-hour repertoire or something, which we had to extend. So we just played incredibly long solos in the middle and the people could not believe it. They'd never seen rock 'n' roll improvisation before. It didn't exist,

★

there was no one else doing it. It happened in a jazz-blues kind of way, but in a rock 'n' roll situation. It was brand new. And it just caught alight and we were immediately successful. And then we realised that we'd actually created something out of necessity because we didn't have enough songs that were good, that we enjoyed doing. And the way we thought about things, we just assumed that it was Jack's job to sing, really.

BATES: **This was the time when the old graffiti started, 'Clapton is God'. Did you get a secret thrill out of it or were you embarrassed?**

CLAPTON: Well, I never actually saw it. I never saw it on a wall anywhere. I saw a photograph in a book once . . . of a dog peeing against a wall that 'Clapton is God' was written on. But I never ever saw that written anywhere or heard people

CREAM IN NOVEMBER 1966 – (LEFT) JACK BRUCE, (RIGHT) GINGER BAKER AND ERIC – 'WE STARTED TO SEE THAT WE WERE RIDING HIGH ON OUR EGOS, AND PLAYING ENDLESS, MEANINGLESS SOLOS'

say it after gigs. I would think that it had just got out of proportion, you know. So I never really believed it. I never believed that it was being said, I never believed that it was being written anywhere. I completely ignored it, really. I was just doing the bloody job, doing it as best I could. A lot of that periphery stuff would just go completely like water off a duck's back.

BATES: **Looking back on it, do you think you were ready personally for Cream?**

CLAPTON: No. I was not ready. It was probably one of the few times in my life when I was completely unprepared for what was going to happen. I had got a picture of what I wanted Cream to be. I was going to be the singer, you know. And I was going to be like Buddy Guy.

BATES: **And did Cream actually live the clean lifestyle that the image was, or was it sex, drugs and rock 'n' roll?**

CLAPTON: It got into that quite a lot, yes, especially with big tours of America. Our longest one was about six months or seven months and in those days there were groupies, I mean fine, good-looking women. It is unbelievable to think that in this day and age, but in the mid-sixties there were chicks who were absolutely beautiful from California and New York, with really nice clear minds, who just wanted to look after you. While you were in town they'd feed you, make sure you had clean clothes and keep you in a good frame of mind. It wasn't sordid — it really wasn't at all. They were just great people. And they would also, you know, turn you on to some smoke or something like that. But the heavy drugs, no, they weren't involved at that time.

BATES: **It's fashionable now to say that Cream were self-indulgent. . . .**

CLAPTON: Yeah, absolutely, oh sure. Absolutely. But I think in a fine way, in a good way. I think it broke up because of that. It was time for it to break up because I think we'd all started to see that side of it. We'd all started to see that we were riding high on our egos and just playing endless, meaningless solos because that's what people came to see. We were not indulging *ourselves* as much as we were the audiences a lot of the time, because that's what they wanted.

BATES: **What I can't understand about you — because you're highly intelligent, quite cynical, motivated — you've got all the things that would lead me to imagine that you would be disciplined in the use of drugs.**

CLAPTON: Ah-ha. I think experience and age have to play a part in this too — and curiosity, creative curiosity, you know. When I started dabbling with drugs, it was out of a need to get on a high in order to play. So we'd take anything. This was happening with Cream. It would be acid, or it would be pot or cocaine or downers or uppers, and whatever, the whole gamut of things. And when it came to the point where I'd moved into the house, I felt this incredible security of being able to do whatever I wanted. The police weren't ever going to come looking for me there. So I used to build up a little cache of drugs. I had a little bit of heroin, a little bit of coke and . . . in a disciplined way I was using it, in actual fact. It was during the forming of the Dominoes that all of this started taking place. We all lived there and we made music twenty-four hours a day and we wrote and we jammed and we played and we had a great life — and we'd occasionally take drugs. The message in this for all of your listeners, obviously, is that there are some drugs that you can probably get away with, depending on your metabolism — in fact, there's no hard and fast law — but sooner or later, no matter how strong you are, they will get you, and that's what happened to me. With heroin, snorting it up the nose occasionally, I really seriously mean occasionally — maybe three or four times a year was how I did it at first. Then I did it for maybe a week without stopping and then two or three weeks not doing it. And then a month without stopping, and then come off and you'd feel bad. So to stop feeling bad you'd take some more, and then you'd be on it for six months. And then, next thing you know, time's flying by and you're doing it all the time. Thank God for me, I was in a situation to be able to afford it. I was loved by people who stayed away and let me have my head in a way, and trusted my own judgement. They did believe — for instance, my family believed — that I would come through and so did my business associates and the musicians too. I saw the seriousness of my money disappearing and the possibility of having to sell things that I didn't want to sell. I was getting near that point. and also that I was destroying Alice's [Ormsby-Gore] life. And we went to see Meg Patterson. . . .

BATES: **How did you find out about her?**

CLAPTON: Through David Harlech — Alice's father. He had discovered Meg Patterson and her form of acupuncture treatment. And then for some reason I just said, 'OK, I'll give it a try', and next thing you know, a very big emotional thing happened to me and I started to really want to live again. When you take a lot of heroin for a long time you cut down on your ability to feel, your sensitivities shut down, you don't feel emotions, you're just completely euphoric all the time so you don't feel pain and you don't feel pleasure. You don't feel anything real at all. But something happened, I suppose some kind of spiritual enlightenment which said, 'Come on, let's see what it's like to be alive again and to feel.' And this big well opened up in me and I did a lot of crying and a lot of self-examination and I went through with the treatment. I stayed with Meg and her family, which was a very important part for me because a lot of that cure was just pure love as much as the acupuncture itself.

BATES: **What was the catalyst that ended Cream or made you decide that's it?**

CLAPTON: I think it was hearing *Music from Big Pink*, if you remember that album that The Band did. It was the first brand-new thing that sounded like what we should be doing, you know, and it made me feel redundant and really stale. I wanted to just immediately go and join The Band or form another band like that.

BATES: **That's happened to you a few times before. . . .**

CLAPTON: Many times, yeah.

BATES: **So that ended and Blind Faith started.**

CLAPTON: I was kind of subliminally trying to recreate The Band in England with Blind Faith. That's why I hung out with Steve Winwood. It kind of changed again from there — and of course Ginger got hooked up with it, which kind of dragged it back a bit towards Cream.

BATES: **Why didn't it work for you?**

CLAPTON: It didn't work for me because the first thing that happened when we got on the road was I met [support act] Delaney and Bonnie and fell in love with them. [LAUGHTER] I wish it wasn't like that. But I was just being true to myself and what musically was the bigger magnet. I mean, it was either: was Steve the bigger magnet or was Delaney and Bonnie the bigger magnet? And the music they were making was a far bigger magnet and I just dropped all my responsibilities as being part of Blind Faith and went and hung out with them. It's not something I'm particularly proud of, mind you.

I started to hang out with Delaney and Bonnie and then I did this tour with them around England and Europe. George [Harrison] came and Dave Mason came. It just became a little circus and was great fun. But I started to feel trapped in this situation too, because Delaney and Bonnie had become very, very possessive of me. They saw me as being a chance at bigger success, because of using my name. There was heavy politics going down within that band [Delaney and Bonnie], and it turned out that Jim Gordon, the drummer, was the spokesman for all the musicians, and was constantly asking for a raise. Jim said that they'd all left, the whole band had left, on account of they wouldn't get the raise they'd been after for a year. They didn't get it and they just walked out, the whole band . . . that was probably Bobby Whitlock, Carl Radle and Jim Gordon, and was I interested in any of these guys? I said, 'Yeah, I'll have the lot of you.' And the next thing I do, I send them tickets and they fly over and they come and live with me at my house. And that's the beginning of Derek and the Dominoes.

BATES: **You were a headline name. Why wasn't it Eric Clapton and the. . . .**

CLAPTON: Oh, because the first thing I wanted to establish with these guys was that, having been through a very strange financial situation with Delaney and Bonnie, the first thing that was going to happen when they were working with me, in order to get the best out of them, was that we'd be on an equal footing. That is to say financially and musically, it would be co-operative. We'd all write, we'd all get paid the same. I wasn't going to take star billing, I'd just be a member of this band. For the time that it worked it was a great feeling just to be part of a band that didn't have a leader, really.

BATES: **How long did it last?**

CLAPTON: I guess three years or so.

BATES: **That's a long time.**

CLAPTON: Yeah. We did a lot of road work under that kind of umbrella. We did a very good album, *Layla*. Unfortunately, it was when the dope started taking hold that everyone got paranoid and the group broke up.

BATES: **Can we go back to the *Layla* days? You did fall in love with Patti. Very difficult circumstance, married to a friend of yours — who's now again a friend of yours [George Harrison].**

CLAPTON: Oh yes . . . never stopped being a friend.

BATES: **How did you manage that? The three of you?**

CLAPTON: Oh, as grown-up as we could, really. The first time I really approached the subject was long before I got into the heroin and everything. I mean I'd fallen in love in the late sixties and it just simmered on and on and on. So it became something that was easy to deal with over the years. You know we would talk about it quite a lot, and George and I would always talk openly about *anything* that we felt about anyone. We've always been very lucky in that he's a really down-to-earth guy and if he sees something in your eye, he wants to know what's going on. So you could never hide anything from him and I would never try. So it was always very much talked about. The person, I suppose, who had the hardest time was Patti because there were these two men fighting over her, but she probably loved both of them equally at certain points of the time. I think I took to drinking very heavy because of the guilt that I felt about breaking up their marriage. I think it was a natural progression. It needn't have got as bad as it got, but I think most of that was because I felt very guilty.

BATES: **You were on two bottles of brandy a day. Again, you see, it's very weird talking to you — intelligent, motivated. You'd been through drugs and you'd cured yourself of that, and yet here you go into being a boozer. Didn't you see it coming?**

CLAPTON: No. You never do with any of these things. You think it's a different substance, therefore it's not going to have the same effect. And when you're drunk, you just don't have any reality, you don't have any reality at all. I don't know when the actual change takes place but at some point, instead of feeling rough when you've had too much to drink, you start to feel rough when you're sober. It can happen over a period of a month, or maybe overnight, but when you wake up in the morning, you feel kind of prickly and alive and you don't want to feel like that. You want to feel numb. And so you take whatever it is, be it the heroin or be it the booze, to get to feeling numb because you don't want to feel pain and you don't want to face life, really.

BATES: **What got you to Alcoholics Anonymous?**

CLAPTON: I was going mad. I got myself there by admitting really that I was going insane. I had double vision and constant thoughts of suicide, especially late at night.

BATES: **You've had a brisk life, I mean, you've had a heck of a life. . . .**

CLAPTON: Oh yeah, twice a life — I'm very lucky.

BATES: **And now not entirely settled, but looking as if you're on the way to getting settled. . . .**

CLAPTON: Yeah.

BATES: **You have a child. . . .**

CLAPTON: Yeah.

BATES: **Are you happy now?**

CLAPTON: Yes, yes, yes. It's a very chaotic life I lead. I don't think anyone really is permanently happy. I don't think I have a right to be happy for more than I . . . more than my just share. And I think there was a time when I thought that happiness was a real bonus for those who were very well off. But I look back at some of the things I've achieved and I feel very proud and I can't ask for more than that, really.

BATES: **The way Radio 1 plays your oldies, you shouldn't need a few quid over the next fifteen years. What makes you run? What makes you want hits? What makes you tour?**

CLAPTON: Just the next time. The next time you play — that's what I look forward to. It's not a great big deal and it really isn't a massive dream. It's a simple experience of looking forward to going on the stage and playing music with people you love.

ERIC CLAPTON ★ 1987	
SINGLES	**REACHED**
Behind the Mask	UK No. 15
ALBUMS	**REACHED**
August	US No. 37
The Cream of Eric Clapton (compilation)	UK No. 3

CLAPTON PERFORMS AT
LONDON'S ALBERT HALL IN 1987 –
'IT'S A SIMPLE EXPERIENCE OF
LOOKING FORWARD TO GOING
ON STAGE AND PLAYING MUSIC
WITH PEOPLE YOU LOVE'

1988

U 2

ANNIE NIGHTINGALE, one of Radio 1's most respected presenters, built up a cult following among millions of listeners with her regular Sunday night show. In 1986, Annie was chatting to U2's Bono backstage at Wembley, when he suggested that he would like to come in to do her show. In the following two years, the worldwide success of The Joshua Tree turned U2 into the biggest band in the world. Nevertheless, Bono, Adam Clayton, Larry Mullen Jr and the Edge kept their promise, and at 7 p.m. on Sunday, 30 October 1988, they arrived at Radio 1 to talk to Annie and fellow DJ, Roger Scott, for what turned out to be their only interview promoting Rattle and Hum. 'Desire' had become their first UK Number One on 8 October, and the film of Rattle and Hum had premièred in Dublin three days before. The interview was a considerable coup, as Annie remembers:

'U2 were absolutely at the top when they came into the show. It was unquestionably the most exciting programme I've ever done, totally live, with no running order whatsoever. They'd said they could only stay for half an hour, but we ended up chatting for at least ninety minutes. It would have been difficult for me to take on all four of them on my own, so Roger Scott's presence as co-presenter was invaluable.

'I think overall the thing that made the interview so special was exactly what makes them so wonderful on stage, and that's the repartee between the four of them, the way the different characters bounce off each other. It was thrilling, and immense fun.'

S C O T T : You must have felt very proud at the première on Thursday night. Everybody stood up at the end, and there was your big night. How did you feel? Larry?

M U L L E N : Well, the Savoy, we used to go there as kids. I was wondering if we get in free from now on. It was great. People in the city went to a lot of trouble. It's sort of difficult in your own city, especially now that the band has got quite big. There's a lot of cynicism, particularly within the press, so on one hand it was thrilling, on the other hand it was a little bit frightening. People think you set it up. It was mixed emotions, and mixed feelings.

N I G H T I N G A L E : Talking of cynicism, there's always the inevitable backlash after anyone's very successful. Did you expect it to happen now?

B O N O : Yeah, actually, we did. It gets boring to say that U2 are great. In Ireland, they've had this for years. And of course there's a lot more things going for Dublin, and for Ireland, than U2. So when they have U2 rammed down their throats I don't blame them throwing it up now and then. I also think it is a very healthy thing to be cynical about rock 'n' roll groups. I think it's particularly good to be cynical about the sort of groups that aspire to the sort of things that U2 do. Because we saw in the seventies how rock 'n' rollers just got incredibly fat on their acclaim, so I actually think it's a good thing. I do understand it, although I obviously would prefer praise.

....

U2 – (LEFT TO RIGHT) BONO, ADAM CLAYTON, LARRY MULLEN AND THE EDGE AT THE PREMIÈRE OF *RATTLE AND HUM* AT DUBLIN'S SAVOY THEATRE – 'DO WE GET IN FREE FROM NOW ON?' ASKS LARRY

SCOTT: One of the things that really came out of that film for me was the sense of danger, of not playing it safe, of taking chances. Was it important for that to come across?

EDGE: I don't know if we'd know how to play safe, to be honest. The band's been surviving on its wits since we started. In the movie you probably see it in a way that you haven't seen up to now. We've got tracks like 'Watchtower' that we'd never played before. It was the first time we played it live, and we put it on the record.

SCOTT: But why did you do that? You were in the caravan rehearsing the thing just before you went out on stage in San Francisco to do it.

CLAYTON: Rock 'n' roll is where you get up on the stage and you do it. I think we felt that there was something that was missing from these long, heavy American tours, that you're suddenly trapped and you can't get on to a stage without millions of roadies, and lights, and PA and whatever. But we said, 'Fuck it, we'll go for it.'

SCOTT: A lot of the recording that you did in the famous Sun Studios in Memphis was extremely exciting because it was recorded live. Bands, as I say, who've got to where you are, don't do things like that. They take two or three years. They hone and they refine.

EDGE: We would do that if we were good enough to do it, but we've never been able to do that. We are not a band who could get it right by spending months. We would kill a song within about six hours, so normally it's the first few takes that have the magic. And from then on, it's terrible.

NIGHTINGALE: Do you still have a backlog of stuff which is going to appear in the future?

BONO: We do intend to basically block up the airwaves for some time to come.

RATTLE AND HUM – 'WE INTEND TO MAKE MUSIC UNTIL PEOPLE ARE SICK OF US'

The sort of mega-album from the mega-band, then the mega-silence, is just too much of a cliché at this point. It's so boring. U2, we're on a suicidal kind of — not physically, but musically — we intend to make music until people are sick of us. We just don't care at this point. We've nothing to lose. All we intend to do is make sure that the BBC sounds like rock 'n' roll for the next few years.

SCOTT: Hear, hear! So how did it feel when you got 'Desire' at Number One? Your first Number One. . . .

BONO: . . . and Bo Diddley was never Number One either, was he? Well, he is now! [LAUGHTER]

SCOTT: It must have felt good, though.

BONO: It certainly did. We wrote it in five minutes, and recorded it in five minutes. It's true. It's a demo we put out. We nearly chickened out of it, but we didn't. It's about ambition, it's about wanting to be in a band, it's about wanting to be in a band for all the wrong reasons, not all the right reasons. People think U2 want to save the world, in fact we want to save our own ass – as well as the world, as it happens. It's about lust – lust for success. We've been in Los Angeles for the past six months, and I met with some very shady characters at various times, and they're doing terrible things in order to survive, and I have to say that rock 'n' roll was our way out. We just wanted a way out. No big deal, no wanting to save the world. And, er – 'Guilty, Your Honour.' 'Desire' is a record of that. It's a beautiful three-minute rock 'n' roll song. I'm delighted that the BBC play it as much as they do.

SCOTT: And I was delighted to hear it at Number One, after so much crud over the year. It was a great Number One.

NIGHTINGALE: What did it feel like after the success of *Joshua Tree*? You had all the classic landmarks, like three Number One singles in America, the cover of *Time* magazine. . . . So did you think, 'What happens now?'

BONO: No, not at all. Couldn't care less. One of the great things about being stinko [stinking rich] . . . [LAUGHTER] . . . is we don't have to worry about any of that. We couldn't care less about the success of our records at this point. We've had one LP that sold so many records that we don't have to worry about things like that again. We didn't even worry in the first place, I must say. But we certainly don't worry now. We're just after music. We haven't made the record that we want to make yet. And we're going to, one day, and that's really where we are right now. And I'm telling you, this is not the band of the eighties. We're just getting it together, just about.

NIGHTINGALE: We've been asking people to ring in with some questions. This is an unusual one. Alan Ivory from Kent: 'What do you think about bootleg tapes being sold?'

BONO: As long as people don't pay too much for them, we've no problem with bootlegs. What I have a problem with is people charging five quid for a record that's, you know, inferior, or a live concert that's been done on a Walkman. They're just extorting people who are into music and into U2. So I really object to them, and I think that they should all have their toenails pulled out. But if they do them at reasonable prices, no problem.

MULLEN: I don't necessarily agree with Bono on this, because I think 99 per cent of it is rip-off merchants. The only system that works is when people tape things and swap them, no one has any objections to that. But when people start selling them on the street, I think it's always going to lead into extortion, and ripping people off.

SCOTT: Let's throw this over to Paul McGuinness, who's their manager. Do you actually go after the bootleggers?

McGUINNESS: Yes, if there are boatloads of them, yes. But I remember a few years ago when there was that stupid campaign that the record industry organised called 'Home Taping is Killing Music'. I remember thinking, 'What a stupid thing to say. How could home taping kill music?' Home taping was spreading music, and I thought it was a good thing. Actually, let me qualify that a little. If there is some bastard in Taiwan who has got a boatload of counterfeit copies of *Rattle and Hum*, and he ships them to Europe, I hope it sinks. . . .

NIGHTINGALE: We have a question from a Mr Davies from Cornwall: 'What are the connections between U2 and the IRA? Does money from concerts go to the IRA?'

BONO: Well, the answer to that is very obvious to most people. And it's absolutely, no, there is no connection between U2 and the IRA. We stand against the IRA, we stand against the UVF, we stand against any men of violence. Our movie is very clear about that. But I will say that I would also be against the British Army being in Ulster. I don't think they want to be there. I don't think they should be there. It's a complex situation, there are no simple answers. But we are against violence, whatever way it manifests itself.

NIGHTINGALE: Does that question shock you?

BONO: It does, actually. I wonder who told that person that. Because that doesn't sound like their own theory.

MULLEN: I remember there were a lot of letters came into the office about that. I think there was obviously something in the press or something.

CLAYTON: It's like someone's not listened to the music. Why are they asking that question?

BONO: I just feel that it is a very complex problem. I sympathise, I understand where they've come from. I don't understand the situation, really, but I can guess. Let's face it, Ireland is a small island off Europe, and the fact that the British government divided it into two countries is a bit ridiculous. I must say, I recognise that. It was a British government started the problem, I would hope that they could find a solution to the problem. But I know one thing. The solution is not in violence — wherever it comes from. And U2 stands against that.

NIGHTINGALE: **We have a live person who's going to ask you a question. Ian Murphy is from Sutton in Surrey. Hello, Ian.**

CALLER: Do you plan to bring session musicians on the road for the next tour? For example, the trumpet part from 'Angel of Harlem'?

BONO: I'll tell you what my dream would be. I would love to take B.B. King on tour with us next year, with his brass section. What do you think of that, Ian?

CALLER: I think that the four of you on stage, the power is just something special. I wouldn't like to see that affected by the backing musicians.

A FILM STILL FROM *RATTLE AND HUM* — 'THIS IS NOT THE BAND OF THE EIGHTIES —
WE'RE JUST GETTING IT TOGETHER'

BONO: It's funny, our manager feels exactly the same way, with his hand on . . . not his heart, his wallet [LAUGHTER]. I must say, that's a very interesting question. If we do take people on the road next year, I wouldn't like it to interfere with what goes on between the four of us, and I absolutely agree with that.

EDGE: So we're all taking trumpet lessons. . . .

MULLEN: It's very hard, when you have four members of a band, to bring other people on. If you bring a keyboard player or an extra guitar player, I think that can definitely interfere. But I think with a brass section, it wouldn't be for the whole concert.

SCOTT: **Now Alison is on the line from Mansfield.**

CALLER: I've got a question for Bono. What is 'tour madness', and how does it affect you?

BONO: Tour madness? It's like cabin fever. I think I talked about tour madness in defence of my own indefensible behaviour in San Francisco, where I sprayed on the sculpture. When you're on tour for long periods of time. . . . Listen, I've got the greatest job in the world, and I'm totally overpaid for it, but that said, there are times when no matter how beautiful your hotel room is, it doesn't matter what hotel it is, at times you start to feel like a prisoner. It's true, and it's a terrible *Spinal Tap* cliché, but sometimes it just brings the worst out of you. You find yourself not going to bed at night, because you can't come down after the concerts. Concerts are everything for me, but basically twenty-two hours of the day are hell, and two hours when you walk on stage are sort of heaven. But after you come back to your hotel room, it's a very lonely place. Even if your mates are just down the hall from you sometimes it's just a very lonely place.

NIGHTINGALE: **Now, Mel from Wrexham.**

CALLER: First of all, I'd like to say thanks to U2 for their music, because I find it very moving and inspiring. Thanks for being one of the few bands that really matter. My question is this — your deeply held Christian beliefs are evident in your music. How do they influence your day-to-day lives as rock stars?

BONO: They really, really confuse us. It's true, I am a believer, and some of us are believers. We are Christians, and yet I don't feel I can say that lightly. I don't feel I'm worthy of the term Christian. I don't feel that I really live up to that. It's a very private thing with us, and we're not very comfortable talking about it in public, because we're only just working it out. So I can't really answer your question, because I haven't really found an answer to it.

SCOTT: **Let's go to Willesden now, and it's Nia Harty. Hello.**

CALLER: Why is Larry so shy?

MULLEN: Why am I so shy? [LAUGHTER] It's not a question of being shy. It's just that it's hard to be something that you don't really feel — this is hard to explain — I don't feel like a pop star. I don't feel like I can articulate myself in the same way as some of the other guys, so I just keep quiet. When I have something to say, I say it. When I don't have something to say, I won't say it. It's just more a question of keeping the trap shut until there's something to say.

CLAYTON: I think Larry is so much better than the rest of us, the only way he can make us relaxed is by being shy.

....

BONO THANKS DJ ANNIE NIGHTINGALE WITH A
HUG AFTER THEIR INTERVIEW — 'IT WAS THE MOST
EXCITING PROGRAMME I'VE EVER DONE',
RECALLS ANNIE

NIGHTINGALE: **Listen guys, it's been marvellous, we've enjoyed it.**

BONO: Thank you. It's a great thing, you know, the BBC. No commercials, it's just the way it should be. We really, really like being here. In fact, when the group first came to London, we used to do these sessions [for Radio 1], because it was the only way to get heard. I just wish John Peel had played us, actually. I called him up once from a phone-box. I was eighteen, I suppose. I don't know how I got his phone number, but I called him up and got through. His wife answered, and I said, 'Hello, could I speak to John Peel, please?' She was very nice, actually. She said, 'John, I think this is for you' — this you'll laugh at, but in Ireland, the public phones don't work the same way, and it was chewing up all my change, it kept cutting on and off — and his wife said, 'This guy keeps getting cut off. I think he's a Paddy.' [LAUGHTER] And I said, 'I am a Paddy! Play our records on the radio.' He never really did put our records on the radio, but I must say still his show is a great, great show.

CLAYTON: I think we should mention that Annie Nightingale kept us warm through many a long night in the back of a Ford Transit van. . . .

NIGHTINGALE: **Really?** [LAUGHTER] **Thank you, Adam!**

U2 ★ 1988	
SINGLES	**REACHED**
Desire	UK No. 1
Desire	US No. 3
Angel of Harlem	UK No. 9
ALBUMS	**REACHED**
Rattle and Hum	UK No. 1
Rattle and Hum	US No. 1

1989

PHIL COLLINS

THE COMPLEAT COLLINS was Radio 1's tribute to the most successful male artist of the 1980s. By 1989, Phil had been an active member of Genesis for nineteen years, and had also had phenomenal success as a solo artist, with over forty-five million albums sold worldwide.

Mike Read's style of interview, informed but casual, suited Phil perfectly. The programmes were produced by Paul Williams and were based on a series of chats conducted at Phil's farmhouse in Surrey. The final update took place backstage at London's Albert Hall, and finished only seconds before he was due on stage.

'Phil does so many different things — drummer, songwriter, keyboard player, producer, screen actor and family man,' says Mike Read. 'He still seems to enjoy them all, and have time for them all. There's all his solo albums, he produces other people like Eric Clapton, and he still keeps Genesis consolidated as a band. He's an amazing character.'

GENESIS REHEARSING AT HEDLEY GRANGE IN 1973, (LEFT TO RIGHT) RUTHERFORD, BANKS, GABRIEL AND COLLINS, 'I THINK I WAS BROUGHT IN AS CLASS CLOWN REALLY.'

READ: **You started playing drums at an incredibly early age.**

COLLINS: Yes, when I was three, apparently. I don't profess to remember this, but apparently I was given a toy drum for Christmas, and I really took to it. Whereas all the other things ended up in the cupboard, the toy drum stayed out. As a result, my uncles, Reg and Len, made me a little drum kit that fitted in a suitcase. That was when I was five years old. So I used to set that up and just bash. I used to sit there in the same room as my mum and dad, brother and sister and my uncles, with *Sunday Night at the London Palladium* on in the background. God knows what it was like for them, but I was just bashing as the programme was on. So from as far back as I can remember, I detoured around the 'fireman, policeman, train driver' sort of thing that some kids wanted to be. I just wanted to be a drummer.

READ: **You also learned to play piano at that time, from your Aunt Daisy.**

COLLINS: There was a piano in the house, but I never really took much interest. I used to muck about every now and then, trying to play chords. But Auntie Daisy, yes, she was a piano teacher. We decided, 'Why not go to piano lessons?' Because she was my auntie, it lasted a little bit longer than it would have done with anybody else. It went on for a couple of months, every Saturday. But the frustration of knowing what I wanted to play, and yet having to go through the rudiments of learning how to play the instrument meant I really didn't stick with it. I wish now in some respects that I'd stuck at it in the same way as I wish I'd stuck at trying to read drum music, because I went to lessons to read drums as well.

All through that period, I had tunnel vision with drumming. I had some friends, obviously, and we used to play around in Hounslow. My dad started the Yacht Club in Twickenham, and I was the youngest cadet. They had annual shows, pantomimes and things, so my drum kit used to come out. There was a guy who played accordion, one who played piano, and I sat and played the drums with them, from the age of seven or eight.

I went to Chiswick Grammar School, listening to Sam & Dave and Percy Sledge and Eddie Floyd, when I suppose a lot of people were listening to Herman's Hermits or The Overlanders. I used to spend Saturday mornings going round the music shops in the Charing Cross Road, looking at drum kits and drum catalogues, and collecting this stuff for no apparent reason. I used to go down there and buy some early jazz albums. I felt I should get into jazz, so I was trying to listen to John Coltrane and Elvin Jones, trying to understand it and not really getting anywhere with it. At the same time, I was buying Buddy Rich albums. Also I was able to go around and buy all the Stax/Atlantic stuff.

READ: **Still you found time to go into acting.**

COLLINS: In 1963–64 I did the Dodger in the West End. It was supposed to be for nine months, but after seven months my voice broke. I loved doing *Oliver!* It was the most exciting thing that I'd done during the whole first period of my life. I started on my fourteenth birthday, and I did acting on and off until I was seventeen or eighteen.

When I stopped *Oliver!* I started doing all the BBC 2 plays and voice-overs, and I had a very small part in The Beatles' *Hard Day's Night*. I was one of four or five hundred kids who were paid to scream at the Beatles. I've seen other people that I know in the film, but I've never seen me.

Eventually, I said to my mum and dad, 'Listen, I've had enough of acting. Really I think I'm old enough to try and find a pro band.' My dad was very proud of me being an actor, and suddenly I was involved in a group, which was all sex 'n' drugs 'n' rock 'n' roll. It didn't have the same kind of thing about it. So I got sent to Coventry for a couple of weeks. My mum and dad were very upset with me. So I started bumming around playing in pro groups and semi-pro groups for the next two years.

I was a professional auditioner for a while. I used to go to auditions and never get them. There was one group called The Bunch who used to play the Marquee quite a lot, and they rang me up from Bournemouth and asked me to go down and audition. I said, 'No, my mother doesn't like me to travel', which is a bit stupid if you're joining a group.

READ: **Your first real documented band was Charge, then Flaming Youth.**

COLLINS: We did this album, a sci-fi cosmic concept album, and I remember it got Album of the Month in *Melody Maker*. It got tremendous critical acclaim, and sold about ten copies, all of which I've signed. I've met everybody that bought a copy of that album.

We went on the road, but we just weren't getting gigs. I read in the back pages of *Melody Maker* that Quintessence always seemed to be playing somewhere, and Genesis used to be everywhere. I remember saying, 'How come bands like these are gigging and we're not?' So, after nine or ten months I'd had enough and I answered an ad in *Melody Maker* which had a square around it which said 'Tony Stratton-Smith requires a drummer sensitive to acoustic music', and knowing Tony from the Marquee bar, I went up to him one night and said, 'I hear you're looking for a drummer for one of your groups.' He said, 'Yes, it's Genesis. They're looking for a drummer, but I'm afraid you'll have to ring Peter Gabriel. He seems to be the band leader.' So I went back home and called him, went down to his house for an audition and got the job. This was July–August 1970.

READ: **When you met Mike Rutherford, Peter Gabriel and Tony Banks, three Charterhouse public school boys, they obviously had an idea what they wanted to do. They'd already released their second album.**

COLLINS: When I joined, it was definitely a very tense atmosphere. I think I was brought in as class clown, really. I was the grammar school, stage school boy. I had the new jokes, and I was a bit of light relief. I think if you ask Tony or Pete or Mike, they'd probably agree with that. I was from a totally different background. I think they hadn't had very good drummers up to that point, and I was a good drummer at the time. I wasn't a writer at all, but I was a good drummer, and they saw that that would be a good plus for the group.

I didn't have anything in common with them apart from the fact that when we did start working together, we all got on great. I made them laugh. I was never made to feel strange at all. There were many occasions when suddenly, out of the blue, Tony Banks would just slam his hands on the keyboard and walk out. I'd say, 'What's going on?' There would be some little confrontation between him and Peter, or him and Mike, or Mike and Peter. There was a lot of tension. I think that was probably as a result of their background.

We did a year as a four-piece without a guitar player, with Tony Banks playing all the lead guitar parts on electric piano. Anthony Phillips, who was one of the original writers with Genesis, had already gone because he couldn't stand life on the road.

READ: **The 1974 album *Nursery Cryme* was the first album you contributed to. It was an era of pretentiousness. Was there some of that in there?**

COLLINS: Undoubtedly. It wasn't seen to be that at the time. We all were seen to be writing things that were a little bit longer than the average pop song. The seventies haven't got a lot going for them. I look back with not much reverence to the music of the seventies.

READ: **What did you feel was your main offering to the band at that time?**

COLLINS: The band originally before I came along were writers not players, and approached everything from a writing point of view. When I joined, I was a much better player than I was writer. My strength was in the arrangement of songs. Another string to my bow was the fact that I could sing, and Mike didn't really like singing. There was a song called 'Harlequin' which we did as a four-piece vocal, but it sounded pretty ropey, especially live. In the end, we whittled it down to just me and Peter singing.

READ: **And you were soon facing the problem of Peter Gabriel leaving the group.**

COLLINS: Peter got more and more involved in writing, first stories, then a possible screenplay. When he did leave it was actually a relief, that we could actually channel our energies full time, with four people that wanted to be in on the band, as opposed to five people, one of which didn't really care.

READ: **Were they thinking then about you being lead singer?**

COLLINS: We were going to get another singer. But by the time we'd finished writing *Trick of the Tail*, we still hadn't found a singer. The studio date was looming, and I was already down to do a couple of songs, the kind of acoustic songs I would have done on the road because I wasn't playing the drums. But the heavier songs, no one had thought of me as being capable of singing anything raunchy. And I wasn't the type of person to say, 'I want the job.' I was waiting for the opportunity if it arose.

Eventually, we went down to the studio at Trident and they put 'Squonk' on and I had a crack, and it sounded good. Suddenly we were a group again. We were self-contained, which is what we really wanted to be anyway. Then, of course, when the album came out we were going to go on the road, so we started looking for a singer again, thinking that maybe we'd find somebody.

READ: **It was very unhip to have a singing drummer.**

COLLINS: I was physically capable of doing it. I used to do it in my school group, but it just looks so awful. We tried to find another singer, and we had the obligatory quick look, and it was obvious that we weren't going to find anybody. So my wife said to me, 'Why don't you do it, and get another drummer?' The other guys said, 'If you think you can do it, by all means, have a crack.'

READ: **Did you think you were going to survive the punk era at the time? Because suddenly the musical world was tilted sideways.**

COLLINS: I think what happened was very healthy. Punk came along and shook this tree and the leaves that were about to fall off fell off, and the strong ones stayed on. A lot of bands hit the dust around that time. We were one of the ones that carried on. I think because there was more substance to us than some of the other groups. We've never really worried about fashion, musicwise or any other way. We've always been about songs, not really about virtuoso playing. Punk really came along and said anybody can pick up a guitar and play, and we were quite into that idea. We weren't a set of virtuoso musicians, as a lot of people thought. We were always put in the bag with Yes and Emerson, Lake and Palmer, and we really weren't anything like that. We just happened to have the same sort of instrumentation. We certainly weren't a bunch of virtuoso musicians.

READ: **The band survived that period, but your marriage didn't.**

COLLINS: Yes, when the split happened, my only way of working it out in myself was to channel my energies into work. I started to pour everything out that I had inside me into songs. The first song I finished was called 'Misunderstanding', which was on *Duke*. If the divorce had never happened, I would never have started singing or writing in the way that I did, which means that Phil Collins solo guy as you see him would never have happened.

1978 to 1980 were dark years for me. I spent a year and a half just writing. I made a desperate bid to patch my marriage up; I was going to go and live in Vancouver, Canada, because that's where my wife had gone. She'd taken the kids. So I said to the guys, 'Listen, if we can record, rehearse, write and I can go and live in Vancouver, and we can still keep this group together, then we've still got a group. But if you can't do that, then I'm off.' So they said, 'You go to Canada for a while, see what happens. We've been thinking about doing solo albums, so we'll go ahead and do that, while you sort yourself out.' That was the wisest thing they could have said. Within two or three months, I was back. It wasn't going to make a difference, so I came back, and said, 'Right, guys, I'm back.' And they said, 'Well, we've started our solo albums now.' So I started mucking about writing, and that's when the *Face Value* stuff started.

Around that time I'd met Jill, who's now my wife, so I was really coming out of the gloom, before I even finished *Face Value*. A lot of people see *Face Value* as a miserable album, but when you actually listen to it, there's some sad songs on there but there's also some quite cynical, tongue-in-cheek songs, saying, 'I'm down, but I'm getting up', lots of songs that are quite optimistic. When I did the solo album, everyone said, 'Of course, it's been a hit so you'll leave the group.' I said, 'Well, no. Not really. The three of us will keep going.'

READ: **You had two hit singles from *Face Value*, a Number One album, and the next album, *Hello, I Must Be Going*, went to Number Two to consolidate it.**

COLLINS: I was worried. I didn't think I had another album in me. But isn't the divorce law wonderful? These things drag on for ever, so I actually did have a lot of things that were still coming out. I think from sadness it went to bitterness on that album.

READ: **Then in 1984, another string to your bow, a chance to go back into acting with a part in the *Miami Vice* series.**

PHIL COLLINS – THE MOST
SUCCESSFUL MALE ARTIST OF
THE 1980S
. . . .

PHIL COLLINS IN A STILL FROM THE FILM *BUSTER* – 'I THOUGHT, "THIS IS TELEVISION AND FILM, IS IT?" . . . I
SUDDENLY BECAME AWARE THAT THIS WAS VERY EXCITING'

COLLINS: They were going through everybody for cameo parts, and they came to the letter 'C' and my name came up. They rang me and invited me to be in an episode, and I said, 'Sure, send me a script.' They sent it to me, and it was by no means a cameo. It was a very big part, and I rang them back and said, 'Listen, do you really want me to do this, because I'm not an actor?' They said, 'Don't worry, learn what you can, and we'll have a good time.' So, I learned the script word for word, arrived in Miami and they gave me a script. I said, 'It's all right, I've already got one.' They said, 'No, this is the new script.' So I thought, 'This is television and film, is it?' I started work on it, and I suddenly became aware that this was very exciting. This was something very different. It was like a rebirth in a way. I had something new. I was thirty-four, thirty-five, and suddenly I thought, 'After all those years of music, this is something else I can do.' And that's what set me up for *Buster*, because I actually came back and said to my agent that I wouldn't mind doing more.

READ: **When the press say, 'Phil's hopelessly unhip-looking', do you go home and look in the bedroom mirror and say, 'Am I?'**

COLLINS: I think I'm wonderfully unhip. Look under unhip in the dictionary and you'll see a picture of me. We've never been fashionable. That's why we kept the pictures of ourselves off the album sleeves for such a long time. We don't look that special, so we therefore felt that a mood should be portrayed on the album covers. I think what makes me appeal to a lot of people is the fact that I am like them. If you actually relate to the people you're talking to, they treat you as their spokesman, almost.

PHIL COLLINS ★ 1989

SINGLES	REACHED
Two Hearts	US No. 1
Another Day in Paradise	UK No. 2
Another Day in Paradise	US No. 1

ALBUMS	REACHED
But Seriously	UK No. 1

1990

GEORGE MICHAEL

S T E V E   W R I G H T   I N   T H E   A F T E R N O O N, *produced by Jonathan Ruffle, was well established by 1990 as one of Radio 1's most popular and creative daytime shows. Drawing on a style known as 'the zoo format', Steve used a 'posse' of Radio 1 staff to create a unique atmosphere of mayhem in the studio. But as the show moved into the new decade, a new element was introduced to freshen up the format, with the occasional and surprising use of 'unexpected guests'. One of the biggest coups was George Michael.*

In an effort to shake off the 'bubblegum' tag which had dogged him since the early success of Wham!, George had become a virtual recluse from the media in the late eighties. But this had only led to more accusations, this time that George and his music were too 'serious'. Talking to Radio 1 on 31 August 1990, George proved his critics wrong as he joked around with Steve and the posse.

'My biggest memory of the interview was hearing continual laughter,' recalls Steve. 'At one point, he declared that he would not be doing any interviews in the future. I thought that was a great shame, because he came across as a very likeable and funny person. In this country the press tend to knock success, and George's problem was that he had become so big that anything he said was likely to be taken up and used against him. We had received the first UK copy of Listen Without Prejudice that morning, which was an absolute masterpiece. If only people would judge George purely on his music, he would be free to be himself in public, as he was during our interview.'

WRIGHT: Were you very unhappy with the Wham! image? I mean that wasn't you at all, obviously.

MICHAEL: Well, within two years previous to that, I'd been a soul boy, a mod, a new romantic . . . I was still a kid, really, so I was still a kind of fashion victim. The pair of us were, I think. But yes, it's embarrassing now. But I can't think there are many people that didn't do anything embarrassing when they were eighteen or nineteen. I don't think I can complain, because I'm here, I'm where I am now, and it's all part of it.

WRIGHT: We've all done stuff that's been embarrassing in our lives. What's the most embarrassing video for you, George?

MICHAEL: Ah, I think. . . .

WRIGHT: I think I know which one you're going to say. . . .

MICHAEL: Embarrassing video . . . so many, Steve [LAUGHTER] There are so many. I think we would probably have to weigh up between 'Bad Boys' and 'Go Go'. There's a great shot in 'Bad Boys' where I'm standing against the wall and the

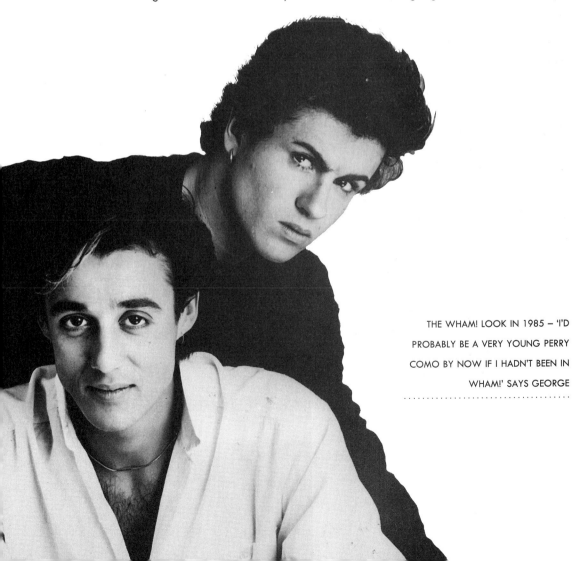

THE WHAM! LOOK IN 1985 – 'I'D PROBABLY BE A VERY YOUNG PERRY COMO BY NOW IF I HADN'T BEEN IN WHAM!' SAYS GEORGE

beginning of the verse goes: 'Dear mummy, dear daddy, can't you see . . . I'm nineteen, handsome, tall and strong', and they just pan up *me* [LAUGHTER] and reveal this real pig, you know. It's true . . . that one was really embarrassing. Then there's the classic shot with the luminous gloves in 'Go Go', which they manage to drag out every time it goes on to a compilation album. I love that one! [LAUGHTER] But I don't know — there are quite a few moments I would take back.

WRIGHT: **They always talk about 'Careless Whisper' as being the classic song. It's like your 'Yesterday', isn't it?**

MICHAEL: Well, it's very strange, because there's something about people's earliest songs. For instance, many people would say that Rod Stewart's greatest song is 'Maggie May', or that Elton's greatest song is 'Your Song', or whatever. There's something about the first time that people get into a studio and make something of their own, and I suppose in a way 'Careless Whisper' was my first thing as a solo artist. I don't know, it just seems to last longer for people. I listen to 'Careless Whisper' and I can see why it was successful, but it doesn't move me in any way. . . .

WRIGHT: **It moves me. Do you know what it reminds me of — of driving along in Los Angeles, with a red sky coming down, and Sunset Boulevard, a blonde sitting next to you. . . . It's that kind of imagery, isn't it?**

MICHAEL: Well, I wrote it in Watford. . . . [LAUGHTER]

WRIGHT: **We had Elton in here — you notice I say 'Elton' like as if I know him — he was in here singing your praises, so was Paul McCartney. I mean, to have praise from people like that, doesn't it blow your mind, George?**

MICHAEL: I think the people that have respect for my songwriting in terms of, dare I say it, older writers, is because I'm very much a traditional writer. So much of the music that's going on at the moment is relevant and contemporary, but won't really stand up out of context. I think I've always written not really for the period I was in. It was always just a matter of writing songs with real structures and melody. Those type of traditional songwriting values are really what I'm into. So I think people recognise that.

WRIGHT: **And what about this whole thing about 'George is not going to do any more videos'? Is that true?**

MICHAEL: Well, there's actually a video idea I've got for the next single, but I'm not going to be in it. I shan't be in any more.

WRIGHT: **It's your video, George, you've got to be in it!**

MICHAEL: I know, I can't explain. But people will probably enjoy watching it far more because I'm not in it. You'll see what I mean when it comes out. But no, I've just decided that there are lots of reasons for me not making videos any more. But one of the most constructive ones is because I want to spend a lot more time writing and recording. I really want to make at least an album every eighteen months from now on. It would have been completely expected in a different era, but I think having been one of the people that's benefited most from video, one of the things that eighties bands have lost because of video is just the need to make music, because you can make an album and release singles from it and promote them for the best part of two and a half years now. And I think it's a shame. When I was a kid, when I had my favourite artists, I expected an album a year, and I had some kind of musical nourishment once a year from them. Now kids have to wait two or three years.

WRIGHT: **Yeah, but with the videos, don't you think part of a rock star's appeal is that people like to feel they know you a bit? So they can see the expression in your eyes, the way you are at the moment.**

MICHAEL: Maybe. I think actually videos tend to do the opposite. Definitely, in my case. I think that what I've written has quite often been at total odds with what's been on screen. For instance, if you take 'Everything She Wants', you can't get much further away from the lyrical content of the song than the live video — of us prancing around. [LAUGHTER] There are so many instances where video has detracted from what I've done, and I think that the more revealing I am as a writer, the less relevant the videos become. Because on video you still want to be glossy and look sexy and all this, and it's just too much of contradiction for me. I'm really not prepared to go out and stand in front of the camera just having fallen out of bed and say, 'This is me, this is how I look in the morning.'

WRIGHT: **Bob Geldof does!**

MICHAEL: I'm not really that keen on many of my videos, actually. I quite liked 'Father Figure', me being mean and moody.

WRIGHT: **You mentioned in one of the songs ['Freedom'] about the whole video thing, the MTV, being projected as a pop star, and it's kind of decrying all of that. What are you going to do in, say, three years' time if —**

MICHAEL: . . . if nobody's buying my records?

WRIGHT: **All right, yeah, if nobody's buying your records.**

GEORGE MICHAEL: 'WHAT'S IMPORTANT
TO ME IS TO MAKE BETTER MUSIC'

MICHAEL: Ultimately, I don't think that's going to be the case. But I'm not stupid. I realise what a large part of selling yourself making videos is, and I realise that the chances are I'm not going to sell as many records. But to be honest with you, it's not as important to me as it was. It's important that I sell records, it's important that people are still listening, but I think having proved I can get to a certain point, basically if that was what worried me, I'd be chasing my tail in a way. What's important to me is to make better music, and to have people respond as though I'm making better music. I'll probably lose out in some sense, but I hope I'll gain in another way.

WRIGHT: **You seem to me — penetrating question coming up — to be more upbeat now than you've ever been, about your music, as a person. You seem to be very happy with yourself. Is that true?**

MICHAEL: I'm quite a happy chappy.

WRIGHT: **Is it all the dosh you're making, or —** [LAUGHTER]

MICHAEL: That's probably got lots to do with it, actually! I'm a lot richer than last time you saw me, Steve. I picked up one of the papers the other day, and I thought, 'Bugger me, I'm worth sixty-five million quid.' [LAUGHTER] Then I thought, 'I'll buy that jumper, after all.'

WRIGHT: **So if you see George in Top Shop on the way home, you'll know he's going to spend, spend, spend. Are you very rich? How do you feel about being rich?**

MICHAEL: I'm not anywhere as rich as I'm made out to be. . . .

WRIGHT: **They all say that, George!**

MICHAEL: . . . but I'm not starving, I must admit. I've made a fair old packet in the last couple of years. I wasn't actually doing all that well out of Wham!, neither of us did, but it makes a big difference when you have a couple of good years in America. So I'm definitely a lot better off than I ever thought I'd be.

WRIGHT: **Some of your contemporaries, some of the pop and rock stars of your era, are now turning to religion, or to drink, and some, you know, go wild with women. Are you turning to any of those things, George?**

[LAUGHTER]

MICHAEL: I don't think I necessarily have to *turn* to any of those things, really!

WRIGHT: **Who do you listen to on the car stereo at the moment?**

MICHAEL: I don't really listen to much that's going on at the moment, really. I'm not wild about what's going on at the moment.

WRIGHT: That's a boring answer, isn't it? [LAUGHTER] I was hoping for something more interesting on that.

MICHAEL: [LAUGHS] Sorry!

WRIGHT: It was going so well, as well. So tell me, do you want to write for any other major artist?

MICHAEL: I think one of the good things about not doing the promotion is that I'm going to get to write more songs. In the past, lots of people have asked me if I'd write for them, fantastic offers, like really flattering requests. . . .

WRIGHT: Who?

MICHAEL: I can't tell you.

WRIGHT: You can tell me, I'm a doctor. . . .

MICHAEL: Let's just say, lots of people. But I've always had to say no, because I've barely had enough songs for myself, let alone to give them away, because I've just spent so little time writing. Now that I'm going to spend more time writing, I should be able to give away more songs, which would be great.

WRIGHT: Do you have any songs stacked up in books already?

MICHAEL: No, that's not the way I write. I don't tend to write a song and then decide whether it's good enough. I get about a third of the way through, then decide whether it's worth doing, and if not, just throw it away. I've got about four songs ready and recorded for the second part of this album [*Listen Without Prejudice*]. That's the most I've ever had ahead.

WRIGHT: Mikey, have you got any questions?

MIKEY WOOLMANS [posse member, Radio 1's jingles wizard]: Yes, is there a song that you secretly wanted to cover, but haven't?

MICHAEL: There's just one song that I've always thought that I'd love to sing, but I had a problem with one of the lines. It's 'Say a Little Prayer'. The second line is 'before I put on my make-up'. And I don't think . . . [LAUGHTER] . . . I've always felt I was cheated out of singing that one!

WRIGHT: George, it's OK for boys to wear make-up. That's what I've heard.

MICHAEL: But generally, if I think a song has been perfectly recorded in the first place, then I don't really want to re-record it. But if something is a recording that

184

you think you could to another way, and it would work that way, as was the case with the cover I ended up doing on this album, then it's worth doing. But there are songs that you wouldn't touch simply because they're perfect as they are.

WRIGHT: **Going back to Wham! for a moment, what's your mate Andy [Ridgley] doing these days?**

MICHAEL: He's shooting around France on a motorbike at the moment — with a shaved head! It's probably something to do with aerodynamics, I don't know. [LAUGHTER]

WRIGHT: **I must say, I met him a couple of times, and I like his attitude. He doesn't seem to worry about much. You know, poll tax etc. — he doesn't care. Is he really like that?**

MICHAEL: Yes, he is. More than anybody I've ever met, he really doesn't care. Generally he doesn't let other people's opinions of him restrain his behaviour, which is great. I'm far too English in that respect. I care that much more, probably too much, about what other people think. Andrew is the opposite.

WRIGHT: **Was that a good combination for the band?**

MICHAEL: Oh, definitely, yes. If anything, the only person who Andrew cared what they thought about his behaviour was me, probably. We had enough respect for each other that we knew as a group that we were important to each other. I think that that was why we were so strong.

WRIGHT: **How do you think it would have panned out if you hadn't been Wham!? Do you think you would still have cut through as a songwriter and an artist?**

MICHAEL: I'd probably be a very young Perry Como by now if I hadn't been in Wham! I would have been far too serious at far too early an age had I not been with Andrew at that time. His attitude was always, 'Lighten up', you know. Which is very good for me.

WRIGHT: **They do say sometimes that you take yourself too seriously, don't they?**

MICHAEL: Oh, absolutely. I take myself far too seriously! [LAUGHTER]

WRIGHT: **. . . he says, grinning all over his face. But do you ever get fed up with that, when people accuse you of being too serious?**

MICHAEL: If I got fed up with people accusing me of anything, I'd spend my whole life fed up, wouldn't I? That's the one strange thing about being successful, in this country particularly. You're constantly defending yourself. And for that to happen from such an early age is quite weird. It's probably one of the reasons that I won't be doing interviews and stuff any more. You defend yourself from teachers and parents from a certain age, then you have a while when you're on your own and no one can touch you, you're independent. But that never really happened to me. I went from defending myself at school and against my mum and dad to defending myself against the press. That's something that's been quite weird.

STEVE AND THE POSSE MEET GEORGE – (LEFT TO RIGHT) JONATHAN RUFFLE, STEVE, GEORGE, RICHARD EASTER, DIANNE OXBERRY AND MIKEY WOOLMANS

GEORGE MICHAEL ★ 1990

SINGLES	REACHED
Praying for Time	UK No. 6
Waiting for That Day	UK No. 23
Freedom	US No. 8
Freedom	UK No. 30

ALBUMS	REACHED
Listen Without Prejudice, Vol. I	UK No. 1
Listen Without Prejudice, Vol. I	US No. 2

1990

ELTON JOHN

REG ON THE RADIO, *produced by Paul Williams, was a two-part Christmas special for 1990, the year Elton had his first UK solo Number One with 'Sacrifice'. Richard Skinner spoke to Elton for the programmes:*

'The interview came at a pivotal point in Elton's life. He'd had a pretty bad time at the end of the eighties, with his marriage breaking up, a court case involving the Sun newspaper, and a drinking problem. When I spoke to him, he'd just sold off all his famous costumes and he was having his house in Windsor completely redone. He seemed to be trying to shed a lot of his past. We met in the house he'd rented in Holland Park, decorated with a strange mixture of genuine Monet paintings and Wurlitzer juke-boxes. There was just him and a butler living there — he told me it was the first time he'd ever lived on his own.

'During the break, he got up and made the tea himself, something the "big star" Elton would never have done ten years before. The interview was about his whole career, and he was happy to talk about anything and everything. He seemed to want to evaluate everything he'd done. He was in very philosophical mood, but also very funny, joking around at every opportunity.'

SKINNER: **The first band you were involved with was Bluesology. Did you enjoy that?**

JOHN: Bluesology used to back Long John Baldry. We were playing a lot of cabaret places up north, like the Fiesta, Stockton, and all those places. I've done it all, you know. Done it all. It was the chicken-in-the-basket set. I became very disillusioned about playing. I was a very introverted man at that time, very, very shy — I wouldn't say boo to a goose. But at least I had the musical integrity to say, 'No, I'm not going to do this any more. I'm not going to play to people who are not going to listen.' And I thought, 'What can I do?' — you've got to realise I wasn't singing at this point. I thought I would maybe write songs. So there was an advertisement in the *New Musical Express* for a songwriter — 'New talent wanted by Liberty Records' — they were going independent from EMI Records. And I answered the advertisement, got a call from Ray Williams, who was working at Liberty at the time. I said, 'I can't write lyrics — '

SKINNER: **Had you tried then?**

....

ELTON IN 1968, WITH LYRICIST BERNIE TAUPIN – 'WHEN WE'RE WORKING,
WE'VE NEVER BEEN IN THE SAME ROOM'

J O H N : No, not really, but I just knew I couldn't. I wasn't interested. And he said, 'Well, I've got this stuff here from this boy in Lincolnshire.' And that was Bernie. And for people who still don't know in this world, Bernie Taupin writes the lyrics to most of the songs, 99 per cent of the songs. He writes the lyrics first and then I write the music and we don't collaborate. We've never been in the same room at the same time. At that time it was very flower-powerish, lots of flowers were mentioned and [LAUGHS] they were very full of imagery, these lyrics. But they were great, and I took them away and wrote some songs to them, without Bernie even hearing them. It just works with Bernie. We just leave it like that because it's worked for twenty-three years and it's been enjoyable for twenty-three years.

S K I N N E R : **During that period, the late sixties, you were doing sessions, weren't you, on other people's records?**

J O H N : I played piano on 'He Ain't Heavy He's My Brother' by the Hollies — we used to have these wonderful sessions up in the studios in Marble Arch. It was wonderful. We used to absolutely cry with laughter. I remember us doing 'Back Home' by the England World Cup squad and that was a classic . . . there was only three of us and — [SINGS] dun-der-der-dun-dun . . . 'Back Home' — we'd just sing 'Back Home' and we'd collapse with laughter. The sessions were a very important part of my life. I sang on a Tom Jones record, 'Daughter of Darkness', and in those days it was all done live. [SINGS] 'Daughter of Darkness', and everyone was crying with laughter.

S K I N N E R : **Eventually you had your first big hit as a solo artist. That was 'Your Song' in January 1971. It must bring a few memories back, Elton.**

J O H N : Well, yes, you always remember your first hit. It was a very exciting time in my life because the *Elton John* album actually broke in America before it broke in England. I made the album in 1970. I used Paul Buckmaster and Gus Dudgeon who I heard do the 'Space Oddity' record by David Bowie and we said, 'We want that arranger.' All the tracks on the album were recorded live apart from the vocals and a couple of overdubs. I had to play with an orchestra, it was very, very frightening. I went to America in September of 1970 to play a club, the Troubadour Club. It was a very famous folk club on Santa Monica Boulevard. The album was a very big turntable hit in America because it was kind of different. It was a lot of arrangements, string arrangements with rock 'n' roll. Because of the dark cover on the album, everyone thought I was going to come out and be very solemn, and of course I didn't. I came out in hot pants, flying-boots with wings on them. We kind of floored them a bit. I got a review by Robert Hillbourn of the *Los Angeles Times*, which was a sensational review, and I became more or less an overnight sensation. It was an incredibly exciting period of my life. I loved what I was doing.

It was all new for me. It was just a wonderful five-year period, that initial period from '70 to '75 when I could put no foot wrong.

SKINNER: **If you could go back and talk to Elton John in 1972, what advice would you give him?**

JOHN: I wouldn't give him any advice. I became the biggest artist in the world and I had a great time. And the naivety, not knowing what to do, was part of the fun of it. I've been very fortunate to be able to enjoy my success, especially in the earlier years. Then afterwards when you hit the peaks and — I was aware that there would only be one peak and then there would be a slackening off — thank God I was ready for it. Since then it's been enjoyable. I don't think I've dedicated myself so much . . . I've drunk a lot in my time and I've misbehaved myself. You know, that side of the business got to me after about 1976 and I became very unhappy with my personal life. I became very depressed and I started drinking an awful lot, and that didn't really help. Some of the music sometimes helps because it brings out emotions, but it didn't help me enjoy the success as much as it should have done. And the enjoyment, I must admit, went out of my life, and the gratitude, because I just wasn't throwing myself totally into the music and that's because I became such a big star. And I'm saying that because I was. I was the biggest thing. Everyone has their few years at the top.

But what it was, I was wrapped up in the whole thing of being Elton John and the whole bit of living the tradition of how to be a pop star. Believe me, a lot of people became very self-important with themselves, me probably included. One of the things that changed all that was the Live Aid concert especially, in England, when people came together and there was no ego involved and people became great mates. It broke everyone's barriers down and since then musicians have played together.

SKINNER: **So back in 1976 were you totally aware of this fact, that suddenly you were on a pedestal?**

JOHN: Oh yeah, absolutely. Luckily I don't think I was unbearable. I enjoy my fame and I enjoy what goes with it, except that the isolation and the loneliness that went with it in the end caught up with me . . . and the travelling. And there was nobody to blame really but myself. I was the one who made the final decision, 'Am I going to tour?' I'm not trying to say it's a sob story, but some of the years towards the middle part of my career, the early eighties, were very difficult years for me because I wasn't happy. The only thing that made me happy was making music and that's really the essence of it. When I got there it was only the music and the love of what I was doing that kept me going.

SKINNER: **You also were developing at this point the more flamboyant side of your stage personality, too. . . .**

JOHN: It caught fire, didn't it really? I suppose it's the result of being a suppressed teenager and being overweight and stuff like that, not really having the courage to do or wear what I wanted to do. But psychologically changing my name from Reg Dwight to Elton John, I thought, 'This is the answer to all my problems, I'm becoming another person', and I did become another person for a long time. I became Elton John, and Elton John liked to wear everything that he couldn't wear when he was Reg Dwight. People used to say to me, 'God, you can't wear that!' And I used to say, 'Oh, you bet.' I was having some fun, because I wasn't David Bowie, I wasn't Mick Jagger and I certainly wasn't Jim Morrison. I was just the guy with the glasses that played a piano, and I thought, 'It's so boring just to sit at the piano and play, with the glasses', and . . . even that became flamboyant, the glasses which I used to wear at the start of the show and by the time I got to 'Love Lies Bleeding' they were so heavy that my nose, which isn't the biggest part of my body — and I'll save that for you later — [LAUGHS] and by that time [HOLDS HIS NOSE] I was singing like that. But everything was still during the honeymoon period and the clothes were very much fun. They got too crazy in the 1980s and I felt uncomfortable. I was too old to wear them and it should have stopped. But again I lost my way a bit as a person. But then in those days, they were real good fun and the people loved them.

SKINNER: **Let's talk about the period when** *A Single Man* **came out. This is '78, the height of the punk boom, Elton.**

OUTRAGEOUS ELTON OF THE 1970S – 'IF I'D BEEN A PUNK, I WOULD HAVE BEEN TAKEN ROUND IN A FURNITURE LORRY TO GET MY HAIR IN IT'

JOHN: Oh, the punk boom. I was sitting in my bedroom, watching Janet Street-Porter's programme on the 'other side' and they had a programme with The Sex Pistols and The Clash and Siouxsie and the Banshees, and they had a go at me. They said, 'Oh, boring old fart', and I actually sat there and I thought, 'Yeah, you probably are.' I liked the punk thing. I didn't like the music much, but I liked the individual expression and I loved the fashion — I was too old to be a punk. I didn't have the hair for it then, unfortunately. But if I'd been a punk, I would have had to be taken around in a furniture lorry to get my hair in it. It was a great era. My music actually was kind of grinding to a halt and it gave energy back to music. It made people like me aware that, you know, that it was fun. Rock 'n' roll is about street music. I'm not a street rock 'n' roll artist and I never really have been. The Who were the street, and the Stones were and the Yardbirds, and people like that, and that part of rock 'n' roll is a necessary thing.

SKINNER: **With all your international success, it must have been quite tempting to move out of the UK, to move your base somewhere else, but you didn't, did you?**

JOHN: No, I did buy a house in Los Angeles in the mid-seventies because I was spending so much time in America and it seemed sensible to have the base. But I've always been a British resident and I belong here. One of the things that's happened to me in the last three years of my life . . . I had an awful year in 1987, personally. I had my voice going, I had my wife and I splitting up, I had lawsuits and it was just everything happening. I couldn't run away from England then because it would have looked as if I was running away from the court case. But since then I went back to work and then I recorded *Reg Strikes Back* and then *Sleeping with the Past*. And from that point on, I haven't stopped working. I miss a base and I just became sort of like a travelling gypsy. I always loved coming back to my home and I miss that very much. I'm a very home-based person. Family, friends and just your own bedroom, you know, 'your own space, man'. I bought a beautiful house in Old Windsor in 1975 and it's still there and it's being redone. That is my home at the moment. It may change but I've missed it a lot. The last three years of upheaval in my life haven't been helped by being on the road. To a certain degree, I chose to run away from situations, not the court case but maybe the divorce, maybe other personal things that were going on in my life didn't help, and when you're like that, instead of standing up and facing it I chose to run away, and the easiest way to run away is going on tour. So that's why I committed myself to the back-to-back world tours. Very long tours. My behaviour on the tours was not good. Nothing's worse than doing tours when you don't want to do them. But I thought that was the answer. I didn't want to go home, I didn't know where I wanted to be. I was very unhappy with myself, I was drinking a lot, I was very depressed and my work suffered on stage. I take great pride in what I do, but some of the nights I cancelled gigs because I wasn't well. I'd run myself into the ground. I was just sick and I became very ill. And consequently now what I'm going to do is just take some time off. I've always been a workaholic and I probably always will be but I *need* some time off to myself and just really enjoy my life at the moment. At this time of my life I want my privacy, and I want to live a much more private life than I have. My life's been an open book to the people around me and although they've really been great to me, my life must change now. You're living in Cloud-cuckoo-land if you think it's a normal life. There have been times when I've just been screaming for privacy but that's been my fault, I could have changed that and I just didn't.

SKINNER: **We were just touching on your marriage that came along about this time, in fact. I think it was the beginning of '84 when you married Renate. And it's fair to say that the press were surprised that you got married.**

JOHN: Not only the press . . . I think everybody was surprised.

SKINNER: **Were you surprised when it happened?**

JOHN: A little bit, yes. I don't really want to talk about it because I know that it would be very hurtful to Renate. I don't regret getting married at all. But we are split up now, we're not together and I know that it would hurt her very much if I talked about it and I don't really want to do that.

SKINNER: **Well, that's fair . . . absolutely fair. Let's talk about other things then, and that same period of time when you were working so hard. You say you were running away from things in a sense and forcing yourself to run the treadmill. What is it in your make-up that makes you want to do that, do you think?**

JOHN: I'm a compulsive person. I just can't do things in moderation, I have to go full tilt. When I said earlier in the programme about wanting to change, I've got to slow down a little, you know. I'm so damned competitive with myself and it's so stupid. This is the time in my life when I should be enjoying a little bit of peace and the things that come with it. Like, I never used to notice the weather. All I really noticed was, I'd get into a private jet and I'd say, 'The seats are the wrong colour.' I'd get into a limousine and say, 'The tape recorder's in the wrong place.' I'd get into a hotel suite and say, 'I don't like the colour of the flowers.' That's what my life came to. Very negative, incredibly spoilt, very ungrateful and, you know, it had come to choosing which flowers you didn't want in your hotel suite. And if there were chrysanths in my hotel suite, I'd change suites. And that is a ludicrous way of behaving and that's why this year I made a conscious effort to sort my life out and seek help. And the worst thing you can do is to isolate and just think you can change things on your own. You can't do that. I used to think I could handle everything. But I'd just put them away, I'd put them on the back shelf and what I did I'd just isolate it and I just became more miserable because I didn't ask for help. It took me sixteen years of heavy drinking to find out I couldn't solve the problem myself.

SKINNER: **A lot of people would have advised you, Elton, following that remarkable *Sun* story that was printed, just to ignore it.**

JOHN: They did, they did. A lot of people in my business, a lot of friends and a lot of artists said, 'Listen, you don't know what you're getting into. You're opening a can of worms.' And they were right. But it wasn't their name involved in it. I had to, you know, it was such a disgusting thing that I was accused of doing that I just had to fight. I remember Mick Jagger saying, 'Listen, think very carefully'; he didn't advise me not to do it. 'Just think very carefully about it,' he said, 'because they're gonna go for you.' And he was absolutely right. When you're naked on the front cover of the *Sun*, it's probably the most embarrassing moment of my life. But I think they were surprised that I was going to fight them. It was a year-and-a-half fight and I don't carry resentments. When it was finished, they gave me the front cover, and the apology was written in the same print and I did an interview with them.

SKINNER: **So we get on to happier subjects here, and 1990 saw your first solo British Number One single. After twenty years.**

JOHN: It's been such a good year for me, this year. 'Sacrifice' initially came out in America and did quite well, Top Twenty. And it was released here and did nothing. Then they changed people at the record company and what happened was that Radio 1, Steve Wright in particular, played it every day and the record company agreed to re-release it. And I said, 'Well, if it's going to be re-released, we'll give all the money away for charity', because it's kind of like cheating. All I want to do until there is a cure found is . . . I can afford to give all the royalties from any future singles to AIDS. It's much better than doing a concert. I'll always be making records and I'll always be making singles and so this is one thing I can do on a constant basis in this country, which is my country of birth, for people who are sick with this disease. I owe them that because I've been affected by it more than anything else. I've lost more people to this disease than any other. Anyway, 'Sacrifice' was an enormous hit and I'm so glad 'cause I really love the *Sleeping with the Past* album, I think it's one of the best albums I've done for a long time and 'Sacrifice' is an important song on that album for me. But for it to be Number One here was so exciting, I was like a little kid. And that's what this business is all about. I mean, I started off saying about being for the first five or six years excited about what went on, then I created my own problems, and the excitement sometimes wasn't there or I took it for granted. But this year's been a major rethinking of the way I am, the way I behave and this was like having my first hit record again. It was so exciting and it was an incredibly happy time for me.

ELTON JOHN IN 1990 – 'HE SEEMED TO BE TRYING TO SHED A LOT OF HIS PAST'

ELTON JOHN ★ 1990

SINGLES	REACHED
Sacrifice	US No. 18
Sacrifice/Healing Hands (re-issue)	UK No. 1
Club at the End of the Street	US No. 28
You Gotta Love Someone	UK No. 33

ALBUMS	REACHED
Sleeping with the Past	UK No. 1
The Very Best of Elton John (compilation)	UK No. 1

1991

MADONNA

MADONNA's appearance at the Cannes Film Festival in 1991 confirmed her as the biggest star in the world. Promoting the film In Bed with Madonna, *a compilation of live performances and 'candid' backstage footage, Madonna's every move in Cannes was flashed across the world on TV and in the press. Simon Bates remembers 13 May 1991 — he was ten minutes late for his chat with the superstar. Embarrassed, worried, clutching his tape recorder in a British Home Stores carrier bag, he arrived at the Hôtel Du Capes to find Madonna sitting on the stairs waiting for him. Once a pot of tea had been ordered, the interview finally took place in her suite overlooking the Mediterranean. The producer was Fergus Dudley.*

MADONNA 'INDOORS', CANNES 1991

BATES: **Where did your toughness come from, was it from your family?**

MADONNA: I think it's a combination of a few things. The way I was raised. I went to Catholic schools for most of my life. My father was a real disciplinarian — very strict, and it was get up every morning and go to church before school, and wear a uniform. When we got home from school, we changed our clothes, we did our chores and homework, we weren't allowed to watch television. It was a very regimented life. I went to public school the last two years of high school — it's the opposite in England, private is public and public is private, I don't understand that. My father was very much into working. He didn't like us to have idle time. If we didn't have schoolwork to do, then he found work for us to do around the house. He thought that we should always be productive and make good use of our time. He was very adamant about that. So I'm sure that had a lot to do with it.

BATES: **Given that, how did he feel when you showed signs of wanting to be, what would you call it, a thespian?**

MADONNA: He wasn't thrilled — because he didn't understand it. My father came from a very poor family. His parents came over on the boat from Italy. He was the youngest of six boys and he was the only one to get a college education. It was very important to him that we went to school and we utilise our intelligence and opportunities. I was offered a scholarship at the University of Michigan. He wanted us to go to school and do the things that he and his brothers never got the chance to do. Me saying, 'I don't want to go to college, I want to go to New York and be a dancer', it didn't make any sense to him. Dancing seems like a hobby, not something serious or something that you could make a living at. He wanted us all to have a good strong educational background, so that we could all be assured of having good jobs and a secure future. What can your father think when you say that?

BATES: **In the movie, *In Bed with Madonna*, is it the real you we're seeing on the screen?**

MADONNA: I don't really think it's relevant how much is me. It's all *me*, but to me how much is the truth and how much isn't the truth, it doesn't matter, because it's all revealing. Whether you lie or you tell the truth, it's still 'telling'.

BATES: **As executive producer, that presumably means you have the first rights of cut?**

MADONNA: No, I gave the final cut to Alek [Keshishian]. All the things that made me feel uncomfortable, I especially wanted to keep in the movie, because I thought these are the things that are going to separate the movie from some other fluff-piece documentary. If you say, 'I want that out of the movie because it makes

★

me feel uneasy', that's the ups and downs of life. If I'm going to show real life, I have to show everything. People are in embarrassing situations sometimes. People are with people and they feel uncomfortable. People can be cruel, people can be funny, people can feel sad. If you cut out all these moments, then what's the point of making it?

BATES: **There's a great emphasis in the movie on being kind and understanding. That's possibly something that people will be surprised at from you, expecting you to be a lot tougher.**

MADONNA: I think you can be tough and still be kind. That's the thing about being a celebrity. You're only allowed to have one attribute. If you're ambitious and strong, then you're nothing else. You can't be sensitive, you can't be vulnerable, you can't be kind. That's just a bunch of bullshit, because nobody is one way completely.

BATES: **When you saw the final cut – at one stage you look really unwell and tired – didn't you wince and say, 'I don't want that shown'?**

MADONNA: Why?

BATES: **Because we all have an ego. I would. I would like to look good.**

MADONNA: Yes, but I've been looking good for years, presenting the best side of me. I wasn't interested in making a movie just about that. I wanted to show other sides of me – the tired side of me, or the silly little girl exhibitionist who takes her shirt off in the room. Those are all sides of me.

BATES: **There are moments in the film where you talk about the tour not as a tour but as a journey.**

MADONNA: The tour was a journey in one sense, that the actual tour for me was emotionally a journey that I took from beginning to end. That's one journey, the experiences that I had along the way, the things I learned. But the actual performance itself was another kind of journey. I think it was very intense, I think it provoked a lot of feelings, and I think it took the audience on an emotional journey. That's what I was saying in the press conference, that that's what theatre is all about. I'm not saying, 'You have to subscribe to this lifestyle', but, 'This is a way to look at life.' Sometimes you have to exaggerate things to wake people up and get them to look at life. That's what theatre is about, in general, it's a larger-than-life presentation of things.

BATES: **You do have problems with censorship. When the movie is released worldwide, people are going to say, 'She's at it again, the showing of the boobs, the going down on the wine bottle . . .'**

★

MADONNA: But everybody's seen that in movies, that's not unusual.

BATES: **But for some reason they take a different attitude when it's you.**

MADONNA: Well, everything is different when it's me, I suppose.

BATES: **Why do you think that is?**

MADONNA: Because I'm very . . . because — I'll tell you what, here's the difference. If some actress or starlet or whatever takes her shirt off, and she's beautiful and attractive, people say, 'I wanna fuck her.' That's the primitive response. When I take my shirt off, they say, 'Is she trying to fuck with us?' Do you

BLONDE AMBITION — 'I WANT TO PROVOKE PEOPLE. I WANT TO CHANGE THE WAY PEOPLE THINK'

know what I mean? Because I think there's something very confrontational about the things I do. Because I'm strong-willed. Because my thing has never been just about being a starlet, some person looking to be discovered by some man to have my chance in Hollywood, or whatever. That's not my personality. I want to effect change. I have things that I want to say. I want to provoke people. I want to change the way people think. I want to assert myself. So when I take my shirt off, it's a different statement. I just do it, and that's it. I think it probably frightens people that I'm so uninhibited.

BATES: **To those people who are frightened by you, and who think, 'My God, my fifteen-year-old son is going to see this, and what will he think?', what would you say?**

MADONNA: I say I think she'd better wake up and smell the coffee, because I'm sure that her own fifteen-year-old son has experienced what that wine bottle experienced. Children are very aware of sex. It's not a secret. I think what's wrong is people say they don't want children to know about sex or teach them about sex, safe sex, sex education. That's a mistake. That's why AIDS is spreading in the heterosexual community very swiftly right now, because straight people think they can't get it. That's bullshit. I think that's why there's so many teenagers that are pregnant, because no one wants to talk about sex. But meanwhile, the kids are all going out and having it. I think it shouldn't be something that we sweep under the rug. I think that we should all just admit that our children are having sex at very young ages, so let's talk about it. Let's talk about safe sex, let's discuss it. Let's sit down with the kids and say, 'Do you want to have a child right now, are you ready to have that responsibility? Would you like to have venereal disease, or AIDS, or whatever?' You have to talk to your children about these things, because they exist, so what's the point of pretending that they don't? It's worse if you pretend that it doesn't exist.

BATES: **When you came over to the UK last year, there was quite a controversy, because on Radio 1, as part of your concert performance, you said the F-word nineteen times. Did you expect the response you got?**

MADONNA: I did it a couple of times the night before, and someone mentioned that all I did was say 'fuck'. So I said, 'OK, if they think I said "fuck" all during the show, I'm going to show them what saying "fuck" all during the show is.'

BATES: **The thing that was marvellous about it for me was that it devalued the word.**

MADONNA: Absolutely. It's much overrated. That's the problem with a lot of things. If people weren't so reactionary, all the things I do wouldn't be so shocking.

BATES: **There's a wonderful moment in the film with Warren Beatty where he says, 'You don't have to film everything.'**

MADONNA: Well, Warren was saying, 'She doesn't want to live her life off camera. Do you have to film even your throat being examined?' But I say, that's not a statement about me, that's a statement about Warren, who's saying, 'I don't want *my* life on camera, I don't want anyone to know anything about me.' He's afraid of revealing himself, I'm not. I made a decision to make a movie about my life, and I said I was going to go all the way with it, and I was going to stick to my guns, and Warren didn't understand that concept. He thinks that if you're a star in Hollywood, you have to have this mysterious aura about you, and if people know everything about you, they're not going to be interested in you any more. I think that's bullshit. You're interesting if you're interesting, and that's all there is to it.

BATES: **But there's a great mystique about you as well, isn't there?**

MADONNA: Yes, because there's no way I could reveal myself completely, or anyone for that matter. You could be married to someone for forty years, and have a very honest relationship, and still not know them completely.

BATES: **You talk about 'mothering' the dancers. I got the impression you are very supportive of gays, that you very much did protect them.**

MADONNA: I probably identify and feel protective about gays in general, because I find them in general to be more sensitive than straight people are. Especially gay men, I think they're much more open to ideas, much more willing to be sensitive. But I also feel their persecution in society, so I sympathise with that, and I feel protective of them.

BATES: **Am I reading too much into it in thinking that in mothering them you might even be a little broody at times yourself, for children?**

MADONNA: Absolutely, yes. The thing is, I've mothered people throughout my life, and obviously I have an instinct for mothering. In my career, what I've done right now is turn it on the people that I work with. But I would like to have my own child that doesn't disappear when the tour's over.

BATES: **Your father is unquestionably the star of the movie. I wonder what in the end he thought of your performance, your show.**

MADONNA: In the backstage area, I said, 'What did you think?' He said, 'It was really good. It was a little X-rated in some areas.' And my brother's standing in the room too, and we tried to explain to him that it's an emotional journey that you go on, and you have to experience this if you want to get to there. He does see it, but my father's a very understated man. He doesn't get very excited about anything. I think he's had to be that way to keep his sanity, because I have eight brothers and sisters, and they're all quite eccentric.

BATES: Is he still a good Catholic?

MADONNA: Yes, he is. And of course I'm a very bad Catholic. I'm not a practising Catholic at all.

BATES: Does that worry him at all?

MADONNA: I think it does, but I think it's clear to him why the teachings of Catholicism are at odds with many of the beliefs that I have. I mean, Catholics are against birth control, they're against abortion, they're against pre-marital sex, they're against divorce, they're against many things. I think that they're ridiculous.

BATES: Does he ever get on to you and say, 'Go on, get in a state of grace today'?

MADONNA: No, he used to when I first moved away from home, but I'm a big girl now, and I think he's realised now that I've made my choice. There's nothing he can do about it. He accepts that. It takes a very special person to do that, and he's a very special person.

BATES: There were moments in the movie when you looked lonely on the road. Were you?

MADONNA: Yeah, because when you're on tour, you live a very isolated life. You go from city to city. The dancers and everybody could go out for walks on the street, and I couldn't. I had to stay in, because there were too many people outside — unless I wanted to cause a riot. So very often I was left alone. But I have my books and my phone calls. It's not that bad.

BATES: In the movie, there's a scene where you're at a press conference, and you're asked, 'Who is the love of your life?'

MADONNA: They said, 'Who is the greatest love of your life?' and I said Sean. And it's true.

BATES: That must hurt.

MADONNA: Why?

BATES: Because to have something that works so well. . . .

MADONNA MAKES AN IMPACT AT CANNES 1991 WITH DIRECTOR ALEK KESHISHIAN (RIGHT)

MADONNA: I didn't say it worked well. Someone could be a great love of your life, but that doesn't mean that you're meant to be together. My marriage didn't work, and I understand why it didn't work, but he's still the one person I've loved more than anything.

BATES: You can accept that?

MADONNA: Yes.

MADONNA ★ 1991	
SINGLES	**REACHED**
Justify My Love	UK No. 8
Justify My Love	US No. 1
Rescue Me	US No. 15
Crazy for You	UK No. 2
Rescue Me (re-release)	US No. 9
Rescue Me (re-release)	UK No. 3
Holiday (re-release)	UK No. 5
ALBUMS	**REACHED**
Immaculate Collection (compilation)	UK No. 1
Immaculate Collection (compilation)	US No. 2

1991

PAUL McCARTNEY

INTO THE NIGHT's *erudite and eclectic style, produced by Paul Williams, was a perfect forum for Paul McCartney to talk about a major step in his distinguished career. In October 1991 he had just released* The Liverpool Oratorio, *his first major classical work, which he'd written jointly with composer Carl Davis. It was a brave venture for the man who wrote 'She Loves You, Yeah, Yeah, Yeah'. Some people were already saying McCartney was being foolhardy, as* Into the Night's *presenter, Nicky Campbell, recalls:*

'When the Oratorio first came out, a lot of people from the classical world were extremely sniffy and said, 'How dare he?' But to my mind, he had pulled it off, and with considerable flair. I think the challenge brought new things out in him. He's a man who is always pushing himself to try different things, and to some extent he's laid his reputation on the line with the Oratorio. Of course, Paul had the last laugh, because the record quickly went to Number One in the classical charts.

'I'm a huge Beatles fan, so I was a bit fazed when this icon walked into the studio and said, "Hello, Nick, I've seen you on the telly." People say he makes an effort to appear ordinary, but I think he's genuinely as ordinary as one can be — if one is Paul McCartney.'

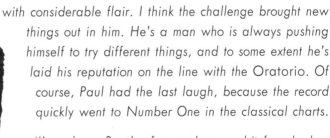

PAUL McCARTNEY AT THE RADIO 1 STUDIO

CAMPBELL: *The Liverpool Oratorio* includes some of the best tunes you've written for a long time. I think it's replete — you seem to have been inspired to write some wonderful melodies. Did you have to fight all the way through to try to stop pop music phraseology coming into it, and concentrate on making it 'classical'?

McCARTNEY: I did a bit of that, but at the same time this was commissioned by the Liverpool Orchestra for a celebration, so why would they ask me if they didn't want a bit of that? And I think Carl [Davis] was often interested in getting that out of me. It is, after all, what I'm known for. If you wanted something different, you'd ask a serious classical composer. I resisted it a little bit, because this was to be my first outing with a straight orchestra for a full work, so I didn't want it to be some sort of pastiche of stuff I'd already written. I was genuinely interested in the form, of this eight-movement idea.

CAMPBELL: It must be a wonderful feeling having an orchestra and choir that size, and people like Dame Kiri [Te Kanawa] performing your material.

McCARTNEY: It was an incredible thrill, particularly because I don't understand music, so it was very difficult for me to visualise all these little dots that we'd laboured on.

CAMPBELL: A lot of people would find this strange, Paul McCartney making a statement, 'I don't understand music.' You're talking about the notation, you don't understand all the black dots. . . .

McCARTNEY: That's what I mean. I can make music up, but I can't write it down. In other words, if you showed me 'When I'm Sixty-Four' or something, I'd be able to follow it mainly by the lyrics, or if I took a little bit of time, I'd be able to follow those black dots. It's not that I'm totally stupid, it's that there's a form of dyslexia comes in and says to me, 'Think of this music, don't just look at it — free yourself.' When we go on tour, I have to learn it all. There's no question of me looking at music, it won't help me. I have to learn all the chords, all the melodies, all the harmonies, all the bass lines, whatever I do. We don't use music. If you talk to a classical person, to go two hours without looking at a piece of music, they find it very difficult. The person I was talking to said he believes the performances are better if you are just thinking it and you know it. For instance, in a lot of Italian opera, people like Pavarotti, they know. But that's how I get on. It's thinking and feeling music. I don't have a fear of it. I'm just very lucky. I've got a gift. If you say to me, 'Do a tune, now', I could go off and in five minutes, I guarantee I'd come back with a tune. It may not be very good, but I have a confidence that I could do that.

CAMPBELL: **Were you worried about collaborating with a respected classical composer like Carl Davis?**

McCARTNEY: I talked to Paul Simon about this, and he said he couldn't do what I've done with Carl. He wouldn't want to give somebody else that much power. If it's going to be a Paul Simon thing, he wants it to *be* a Paul Simon thing. He wants absolute control over everything. I don't really have that problem. I like collaborators. I was very keen on this thing, so I was giving it my all. I was definitely trying to write something that would stand up as a repertoire piece for orchestras. And as you say, with me not knowing the notation and stuff, I had to be quite careful, because it could have just been a chasm that I didn't know I was falling into. Whereas in actual fact, I never felt like that. I thought, 'Look, I don't know the rules, but I know what harmony is, I know what atonal music is, I know what tempos are.' In fact, I hate to tell you, but some of the people in rock 'n' roll have got a better understanding of tempos than a lot of classically trained people.

CAMPBELL: **Did you regard it as more serious, what you were doing?**

McCARTNEY: There is some element where when you're dealing with soloists, a chorus, pages of written music, and a full orchestra, there is some way that I think you could perceive it as being more serious than rock 'n' roll. We're a bit more light-hearted — but we're able to be, because the inspiration in rock 'n' roll comes from the inter-reaction in the group. So I can throw my guitarist a solo, and say, 'Go on, it's in A. Do me something', which they just don't tend to do outside of rock 'n' roll and jazz.

CAMPBELL: **More's the pity.**

McCARTNEY: But I felt quite comfortable about doing it, because I think there's this seriousness and this stuffiness that has become attached to things like opera that's not necessary, because really it's all just a bunch of music. These traditions have grown up, and they make us frightened of it. I think that's the worst thing about it.

CAMPBELL: **In the old days, you'd cite Chuck Berry and Elvis and Buddy Holly as your influences. What were your influences for this oratorio?**

McCARTNEY: That was one of the nice things about it. Coming into rock 'n' roll, I did know these people you're mentioning, and I knew their work as a fan. Because before I got into a band, I was just a record-collecting, card-carrying fan. Coming into the classical world, the excitement was that I didn't know anything. I know some Bach pieces, I know — [hums Toccata and Fugue in D Minor] — and all that sort of stuff. I know what I've picked up over the years, where you know what you like.

You think, 'What's that one? It's not the cigar commercial, what's it really called?' And that was really the extent of my knowledge. So, it was really good. I had to do things like go and listen to an orchestra. So I went to the Proms about two years ago, and listened to them playing whatever they were playing — it happened to be Dvořák. I picked up little bits of information like that. I would just happen to hear an orchestra on the radio, and a solo violin would come in, and I wouldn't really know what the piece was, but I'd think, 'Oh, I love solo violin.'

CAMPBELL: **Was this for the specific purpose of actually getting your ears in tune with what can be done with an orchestra?**

PAUL McCARTNEY CELEBRATES WITH CO-WRITER CARL DAVIS AT THE PREMIÈRE OF *THE LIVERPOOL ORATORIO* — 'IT WAS AN INCREDIBLE THRILL — PARTICULARLY BECAUSE I DON'T UNDERSTAND MUSIC'

McCARTNEY: Yes, I had to see what they had and what they could do. And I must admit, I probably unconsciously nicked things from that Dvořák piece. We used to do a lot of that with The Beatles. For instance, the introduction on 'Here, There and Everywhere'. I remember in the studio, we'd say, 'Let's make it like The Beach Boys.' So, you know, we'd go [SINGS] 'Ooh, to lead a better life. . .'. Of course, it doesn't sound anything like The Beach Boys, but you just use them as a sort of mascot, as a little icon, to tune in on. And I did that kind of thing with the *Oratorio*. I'd come back to Carl and say, 'I've just heard this composer, and it seemed to me that he was trying to not arrive', like it's a bit of a tease. All it did was make me think, 'Oh, that's a good idea.' Because I always try to 'arrive'. If you think of something like 'Can't Buy Me Love', it starts off [SINGS] 'One, two, three, can't buy me love . . .' and you've arrived. With the first word you're in there with the hook. Whereas, with the classical composers, often they'll try and keep you waiting, they'll pass it round the orchestra, for instance. So it was more that than specific composers.

CAMPBELL: **It was the way they did things, rather than what they did.**

McCARTNEY: I noticed them as if they were contemporary writers. I'd think, 'What's he doing here?' So, OK, the cigar ad [Air on a G String], he's got a lovely descending bass line, then he's got this very beautiful melody played against it. That's very simple composition. So I just nicked how he did it. I'd think, 'OK, well, that's the ball game, now I'll put my melody on top of, let's say, an ascending bass line.' I'd just use things to get me into the ball park, then I'd try and be original once I'd got there.

CAMPBELL: **Is any of this going to manifest itself on your next pop album? Has this been a musical education for you?**

McCARTNEY: It really has, actually. That was one of the great things about it. As we were doing it and putting it together, I felt very good about the idea of structuring it. On the new album I've been writing for a while, what I've done for the first time in a long time, is that I've actually got all the songs written, all the words so that I'm happy with them, they're all in an order. I've actually laid out the album before I've recorded a single thing. I don't know if it's going to work or not, there's no guarantee this'll make a better album, but in my mind, I feel a lot better about it, because I really feel I've got some strong songs. And if we open with a rock 'n' roll one, I'll know what the next one ought to be. So I know where I am a bit more. Whereas we normally just come together with a handful of songs, pull them out of the bag and do whichever one we feel like doing.

CAMPBELL: **Is there any disenchantment with the pop music business? Did that perhaps lead you to other things and give you an extra impetus?**

McCARTNEY: No, not at all. It was just the excitement of doing something new. It wasn't that I was bored.

CAMPBELL: **But the singles market is very, very. . . .**

McCARTNEY: It's strange at the moment, isn't it? It's very small, I agree. It's strange. You've either got something like the Bryan Adams thing ['Everything I Do'], that sort of anthemic thing that sticks around for ever, then there's all these little 'schuck-a-schuck-a' disco records flashing through.

CAMPBELL: **I thought you might have a feeling of wanting to try something else.**

McCARTNEY: Well, I do have a feeling of that, but it didn't propel me into saying, 'Oh my God, I've had enough of this.' In fact, the opposite. I'm really looking to getting back to what I do as the main string to my bow. We were rehearsing this week with the band, and it is great to wind the amps up and hurt your ears again. I like the idea of it being a balance. Because I do love both things.

CAMPBELL: **Are both things going to continue, then?**

McCARTNEY: That's how I'd like to do it. When you think about the Beatles, some people think about 'rebellious' rock 'n' roll, you think of that kind of image. But then when you actually examine what we did, things like 'Eleanor Rigby', that's almost a classical record right there: there's no rock 'n' roll instruments on it, it's all fiddles. It's just a bunch of string players. The only pop thing is that it's double tracked.

CAMPBELL: **But you'll no doubt be using some of these classical techniques that you've learned. Like, for example the jarring chords.**

McCARTNEY: Yes, I'm interested in that stuff. That's one of the things that classical music does that's in a way more exciting than what rock 'n' roll does. If rock 'n' roll wants to be weird, it just gets louder or more aggressive, or the lyrics swear at you or something. In classical music, say you're in C, you can take something from a completely other key, and scream across it. You get a sense of film music, like the *Psycho* stuff, those *Psycho* strings, set against each other, the sort of jarring on purpose. I like that.

CAMPBELL: **There's a jarring chord in 'Long and Winding Road', isn't there? It's the eleventh, I think.**

McCARTNEY: I don't know! Don't ask me, I just write them. It's just something I found on the piano. It's a nice little combination, that. But I'm still discovering all of that. It's one of the joys. People say to me, 'Why are you still in music? You've made your money, why don't you sod off and go on holiday?' But I'm still fascinated

— finding out things on the piano. And one of the great things about this, I've now realised, you can put anything with anything. It won't always work, but it's a great thing to try. Because as a rock 'n' roll artist, I'm constricted. It's like I run in blinkers, I'm a racehorse in blinkers. I know what I know, and I've developed a system of how to write 'McCartney' kind of stuff. But this was good for me — it took off the blinkers. An orchestra makes a different sound from a band. If you've got Julian Lennon, for instance, and his band, and they play this grinding, atonal chord, you probably think he's made a mistake. If you put that writing on to violins, it sounds beautiful and sweet. It's something to do with the nature of the instrument. I think that's quite exciting.

CAMPBELL: **One of the things people say about Paul McCartney is that he's a great melodist. When Andrew Lloyd Webber came into this show, he named the four greatest melodists of the twentieth century, and you were one of them. You were in there with Puccini. But one of the things about McCartney songs is the simplicity of them, and there's great virtue in simplicity. One of my favourite Beatles songs is 'I Will', which nobody ever talks about, on the *White Album*. A song like that, how did that come about?**

McCARTNEY: I can't tell you how they come about. I just sit down when I'm in the mood, and I grab a guitar, and I get lucky. I just hit some chord that interests me. It's those opening chords.

CAMPBELL: **You've written this oratorio, classical music, but a lot of people say that the Beatles is the classical music of the future. McCartney songs are the classical music of the future.**

McCARTNEY: Well, Lennon and McCartney things, I think, in particular, not just mine. I used to argue with people about that. I used to say, you know, 'Autumn Leaves' and 'Hello Dolly', you think of them as your standards. I said there will come a time when there will be certain Beatles songs you will think of as your standards. But at the time we talked about it, it was very hard to imagine that happening with Beatles stuff. It's now easier to imagine. I mean, my kids come home from school, and in their history books, there's 'The Beatles', 'The Sixties', 'The social phenomenon'. It did occur to me, seeing as we were in all those things whether I like it or not, we were part of that 'sixties' scene, it always amuses me to think, like with Queen Elizabeth I you always think of Raleigh, or somebody like that, with Queen Elizabeth II, you're going to think of The Beatles. In her reign, we've been a fairly big phenomenon. And the great thing is, she's aware of it.

CAMPBELL: **I remember my first memory of the Beatles was watching 'Hey Jude', I think on *The David Frost Show*, in about 1968. I was about seven years old. I remember my mother criticising the other three, but saying, 'Oh, Paul McCartney, he's the nice one.'**

McCARTNEY: [LAUGHS] If only they knew.

CAMPBELL: **But musically too, you were the nice guy, and sometimes the rebel. You did produce quite a broad range, didn't you? From 'Helter Skelter' to 'Honey Pie'.**

McCARTNEY: I've always kind of wondered about that. In one way, I could be seen to be a Jack of all trades, master of none, 'God, I haven't got a style that's mine', but I've given up worrying about that stuff now. I've done it now, it's all spilt milk. And I'm certainly not going to worry about the stuff I'm going to do from now on. The thing was always to try and enjoy yourself. If you can actually enjoy making records, actually enjoy working with John Lennon, enjoy playing a guitar solo with George Harrison, somehow it communicates itself. That really is the only philosophy I've decided to go with. OK, it may be a bit of a jump from 'Helter Skelter' to 'Honey Pie', but rather than sort of – as Linda would say – 'whipping myself with a soggy noodle', I don't see there's any point in that. There's enough people around in life to help you. I try and give myself a good time. It's so easy to get negative about yourself. People are very surprised to hear me talk like this. They say, 'You couldn't get negative about yourself, you wrote "Yesterday". How could you ever think you're not a good songwriter?' But believe me, it's very easy. I'm sure anyone who's ever tried to do anything, and is recognised for doing it . . . I certainly know John Lennon was quite insecure about himself, and there's a giant from the twentieth century, John was definitely no slouch. Certainly in my book, he's one of the geniuses of the twentieth century. But he was insecure about himself. But that leads me to believe that everyone is. There's no such thing as a confident person. So I try to just get on with it, and just enjoy what I do.

1992

ANNIE LENNOX

A N N I E L E N N O X was half of one of the most successful and creative groups of the 1980s, the Eurythmics. In February 1990, she announced on Radio 1's Simon Bates Show that she was taking two years off. After that, while her musical partner, Dave Stewart, went his own way, very little was heard of Annie. She had a baby, Lola, and was said to have been working for Shelter, the charity for the homeless. In 1991, Eurythmics' Greatest Hits became the UK's second bestselling album of the year, and the duo seemed to have been placed firmly in the back catalogue of the collections of the new CD generation, between the Doors and Fleetwood Mac.

Then in the spring of 1992, Radio 1 got word of an exciting new development – Annie was preparing her first solo album. As ever, she would only be doing a few interviews to promote it. One of them would be for Paul Gambaccini, who, along with producer Kevin Howlett, went to talk to Annie on 3 March about the album, Diva, and about her career to date.

'Eurythmics had led the second British invasion of the US in 1983/84, but they were the only ones from that period who matured and sustained the decade,' remembers Paul. 'I'd known Annie Lennox since the early days of the Tourists, and seen her and Dave achieve immense success. But the Annie I found in 1992 was a person who had eliminated all the excesses that success in the rock industry can bring. She'd got rid of all the unnecessary anxiety, and she'd created a great dignity around herself. I'd always been struck by her honesty in interviews, and her courage both as a person and as an artist, and these were qualities which were still evident as we talked.'

GAMBACCINI: We're here to talk about *Diva*, Annie Lennox's first solo album. Annie, in your own words, why?

LENNOX: I'd never harboured any strong desire to be a solo performer, outside of Eurythmics, because I felt so artistically satisfied in that set-up. But, as you said, I took two years off, because it was the right thing to do at that point. I had constantly been making records and touring. Actually, that period of time lasted for about fifteen years really, because before Eurythmics, Dave and I were in another group and we did all of that. And in a way, I needed to stop. I didn't want to give up music, but I wanted to reclaim myself, if you like. I also wanted to start a family, and I've been very fortunate in that my daughter's now about fourteen-months old, and all that has been taken care of safely. Actually, while I was expecting her, I had the possibility to think about my situation as to whether I wanted to continue in music and how I would do it. It became apparent to me that music was a very important part of my life, and that I was so strongly caught up and self-identified with music, that it would have been very hard for me to say simply, 'That's it, I'm finished with it now.' It wasn't the right thing to do. So I decided that I'd write some songs, and try to approach making a record in a very gentle way, with no pressure. There was no pressure from any record company person or anybody actually. I just quietly came back to it, in a sense refreshed and with the right kind of motivation in mind. Also, I wanted to find out where my musicality lay, where my own statement would be. I didn't really know, so in a way it was a time of self-discovery in a musical sense.

ANNIE WITH DAVE STEWART IN THE EARLY DAYS OF EURYTHMICS — 'UP TO A FEW YEARS AGO,
EURYTHMICS WAS ALWAYS MY NUMBER ONE GOAL IN LIFE'

GAMBACCINI: **You mentioned that while you were expecting Lola, you contemplated the possibility of giving up music altogether. Was that really a serious possibility?**

LENNOX: Oh, yes, definitely. Because I've lived through the music, if you like, for such a long time, and I do realise how all-consuming that lifestyle is. I mean once a group becomes successful, the momentum of that success is enormous. You're faced with tours that will take you off around the world for ever. For example, Eurythmics really could have sold Wembley Stadium at least twelve times and more, and it just seemed to us that it just never seemed to stop. People say to you, 'Oh, groups get big and they turn into stadium bands and the reason they do that is because if they were to play to everybody in small theatres, they'd be stuck there for months. So in practical terms, you have to get around the world, you have to play to people. And then, of course, you come up against these limitations. And ultimately, you have to stand back, you have to think about what it means to you. I think that I had started to value my private life more than Eurythmics. Up to a few years ago Eurythmics was always my number one goal in life — not the money, not the success — essentially making the music, and making good music. That challenge has always been what spurred me on, and it still is.

GAMBACCINI: **Were you personally surprised by the extent of the success of the *Greatest Hits* album?**

LENNOX: The music was never made for the money, but when a lot of people go out and buy your record, it says something, you know. I think the beauty of the *Greatest Hits* album is that it does so beautifully illustrate the cross-section and the diversity of Eurythmics music in one record. It has something that can appeal to everybody, and I'm sure that most people that buy albums will probably have the *Greatest Hits* in their collection, and for me that is incredibly flattering. It really says something about what Eurythmics meant to people or means to people.

GAMBACCINI: **You've said that Stevie Wonder's music has been very important to you, with 'My Cherie Amour' and his *Talking Book* album.**

LENNOX: Absolutely. At the time I was listening to those records, I had no idea that I was probably preparing myself for a future as a singer. I just knew that I loved singing, and I instinctively used to sing the songs that I loved — on my own, I don't mean singing to audiences. I would sing in the kitchen where the acoustics might be quite good or wherever. I was actually practising. I was putting down the foundations of a vocal style.

GAMBACCINI: **It's very amusing to our listeners that you went to the Royal Academy of Music — but not as a vocalist.**

LENNOX: It's very amusing to me too, actually. I should never have gone there. It was a total mistake. I went there to study the flute. Girls from provincial towns don't historically get into groups. Maybe now it's a little bit different, but the only way of getting into music for me then was to play. And the music that was being made was in school, in orchestras and chamber groups and things — it was classical. I'd never had the possibility in my mind that a girl could write songs and sing. It really wasn't until I heard Joni Mitchell actually, when I saw this woman who writes poetic lyrics, which were so unique for their time, and who sings them in this extraordinary way, that I thought maybe I can do that. So she was a sort of example for me, of a possibility, and once that possibility had sunk in, very deeply, and resonated so strongly with me, I understood that that was what I should be doing, in a very deep sense. I realised that I wanted to sing. Actually, that was it. It started from that. I had no doubts about it.

GAMBACCINI: **The way 'Sweet Dreams' took off in America is quite fascinating, because it took months, literally, but it did become a Number One record. And of course it made it seem as if you had come from nowhere, when in fact you had been struggling for years. What do you find is the difference in the treatment you've had in America and in the UK?**

LENNOX: Well, America is a strange animal for me, the American culture is a strange phenomenon that I don't particularly identify with. I would say that the American chart is very formulated. Either you are heavy metal, or you're country, or you're soul, or you're R&B — people all fall into these categories. It seems to me that people like myself, and like Eurythmics and many other groups who don't fall so neatly into those categories, people in America don't know what to do with you. They don't know what to call you. They don't know what to label you. And this confounds their imagination in a way, they can't handle it.

GAMBACCINI: **It's almost amusing that one of your three biggest hits in the States, along with 'Sweet Dreams' and 'Here Comes the Rain Again', would be 'Would I Lie to You?' which is an out-and-out, almost metally rock record.**

LENNOX: Yes, that's right. I think the trouble with us is that we always wanted to progress. We always wanted to make a move forward, and if our tendency was to want to make more hard-edged, rock-orientated music at the time, then suddenly we were a rock group. Then the next record we made after 'Revenge' — I think it was 'Savage' — this completely confused everybody. They'd say, 'We thought you were a rock group, what are you now, an art group?' For me, it's really important not just to stand in one space. When you're creative, you have to take risks. You have to risk the fact that you may alienate your audience. But you're going to have to take that risk, because if you don't you're going to be compromising yourself, compromising your musicality, and going backwards and becoming sterile and stagnant.